THE IRISH
COAST TO COAST WALK

About the Author

Paddy Dillon is a prolific outdoor writer with 30 books to his name, as well as a dozen booklets and brochures. He writes for a number of outdoor magazines and other publications, as well as producing materials for tourism groups and other organisations. He lives on the fringe of the Lake District, and has walked, and written about walking, in every county in England, Scotland, Ireland and Wales. He generally leads at least one guided walking holiday overseas every year and has walked in many parts of Europe, as well as Nepal, Tibet and the Canadian Rockies.

While walking his routes, Paddy inputs his notes directly into a palm-top computer every few steps. His descriptions are therefore precise, having been written at the very point at which the reader uses them. He takes all his own photographs and often draws his own maps to illustrate his routes. He has appeared on television, and is a member of the Outdoor Writers' Guild.

Other Cicerone guides written by Paddy include:

Irish Coastal Walks	Walking in County Durham
The Mountains of Ireland	Walking the North Pennines
Channel Island Walks	GR20 Corsica: High Level Route
The Isles of Scilly	Walking in Madeira
Walking in the Isle of Arran	Walking in the Canaries: Vol 1 West
Walking the Galloway Hills	Walking in the Canaries: Vol 2 East
The South West Coast Path	Walking in Malta

THE IRISH COAST TO COAST WALK

by
Paddy Dillon

2 POLICE SQUARE, MILNTHORPE, CUMBRIA LA7 7PY
www.cicerone.co.uk

© Paddy Dillon 2005

First edition 1996 (ISBN 1 85284 211 3)
Second edition 2004

ISBN 1 85284 433 7

A catalogue record for this book is available from the British Library

Dedication

To the memory of J. B. Malone

Advice to Readers

Readers are advised that while every effort is taken by the author to ensure the accuracy of this guidebook, changes can occur which may affect the contents. It is advisable to check locally on transport, accommodation, shops, etc, but even rights of way can be altered. Paths can be affected by forestry work, landslip or changes of ownership.

The author would welcome information on any updates and changes sent through the publishers.

Front cover: Walkers next to J. B. Malone's memorial stone, high above Luggala

CONTENTS

Introduction 9
Coast to Coast Geology 11
Irish Weather 13
Irish Flowers and Animals 14
Access to the Countryside 16
Route Finding 17
Map Coverage 18
Travel to Ireland 19
Getting around Ireland 20
Accommodation 20
Food and Drink 23
Money 23
Tourist Information Offices 25
When to Walk 25
One Man and his Dog 27
Daily Schedule 27
Emergency Services 28

Stage 1: The Wicklow Way 29
Day 1: Dublin to Marlay Park 30
Day 2: Marlay Park to Knockree 38
Day 3: Knockree to Laragh 43
Day 4: Laragh to Glenmalure 51
Day 5: Glenmalure to Tinahely 59
Day 6: Tinahely to Clonegal 64

Stage 2: The South Leinster Way 69
Day 7: Clonegal to Borris 70
Day 8: Borris to Inistioge 76
Day 9: Inistioge to Mullinavat 83
Day 10: Mullinavat to Carrick-on-Suir 88

Stage 3: The East Munster Way 94
Day 11: Carrick-on-Suir to Clonmel 95
Day 12: Clonmel to Newcastle 101
Day 13: Newcastle to Clogheen 105

Stage 4: The Blackwater (Avondhu) Way 110
Day 14: Clogheen to Araglin 111
Day 15: Araglin to Fermoy 115
Day 16: Fermoy to Killavullen 121
Day 17: Killavullen to Bweeng 128

Stage 5: The Blackwater (Duhallow) Way 134
Day 18: Bweeng to Millstreet 135
Day 19: Millstreet to Shrone 142
Day 20: Shrone to Muckross 149

Stage 6: The Kerry Way 152
Day 21: Muckross to Black Valley 153
Day 22: Black Valley to Glenbeigh 159
Day 23: Glenbeigh to Cahersiveen 166
Day 24: Cahersiveen to Portmagee 172

Leaving the Irish Coast to Coast Walk 178

High-level Alternative Routes 179
The Lug Walk 180
Blackstairs Mountains 185
Comeragh Mountains 188
Knockmealdown Mountains 192
Derrynasaggart Mountains 195
MacGillycuddy's Reeks 198
Coomasaharn Horseshoe 202

Appendices
Appendix A: Glossary of Common Irish Words 205
Appendix B: Irish Coast to Coast Walk Accommodation List 208
Appendix C: Route Summary Table 217

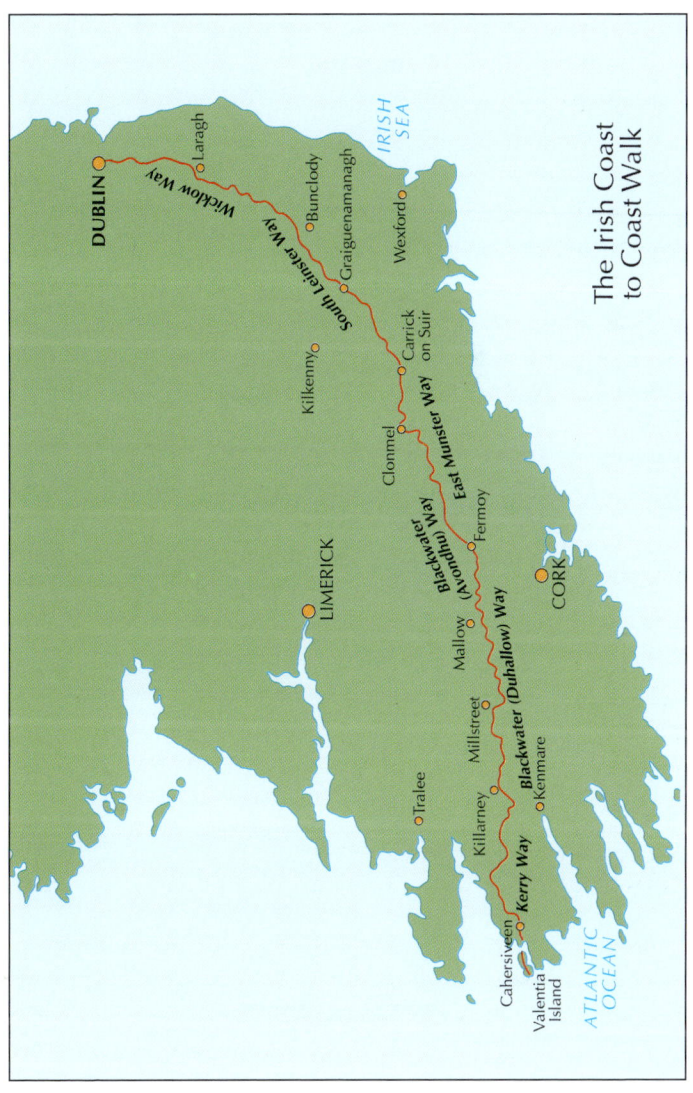

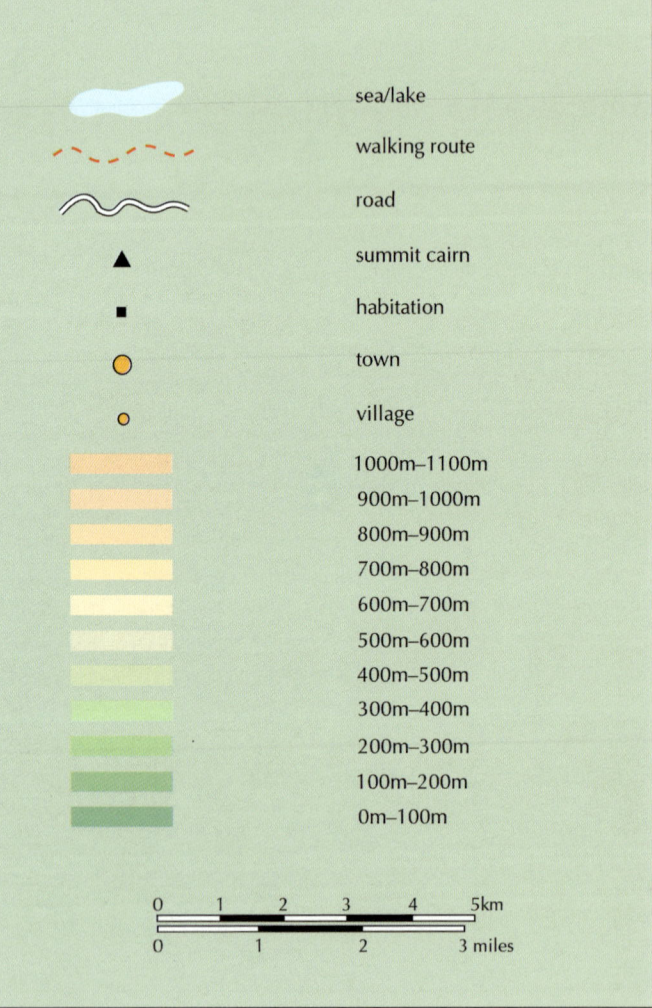

INTRODUCTION

Waymarked long-distance walking routes are a relatively recent addition to the Irish countryside. The Wicklow Way was the first such trail to be fully marked and offered to walkers, and it was soon connected with other waymarked trails to offer a Coast to Coast Walk across Ireland from the heart of Dublin to the Atlantic cliff coast of Co Kerry.

Much of the credit for initiating the development of the waymarked trail network must go to the late J. B. Malone; often referred to as the 'Walking Encyclopedia', JB took to the hills in 1931 and contributed articles about walking to the *Evening Herald* newspaper from 1938 to 1975. The Wicklow Mountains were the hills he knew and loved best, and in 1966 he prepared a plan for a route that was to become the Wicklow Way. Originally he envisaged a circular walk, but Cospoir (the National Sports Council) became involved in the development of walking routes and the Wicklow Way became a linear plan so that it could link with a proposed South Leinster Way. This was in turn planned to link with other trails, including the Kerry Way in the south-west of Ireland. The Wicklow Way was declared open in 1982 and other routes followed in turn. JB was appointed as Field Officer by Cospoir and he was closely involved in the

A frosty scene near Brewsterfield, looking towards the rugged mountains (Day 20)

development of the early waymarked trails. A stone above Luggala in the Wicklow Mountains commemorates him as the 'Pioneer of the Wicklow Way' – a picture of this stone appears on the front cover of this guidebook.

Problems with the waymarked trails arose almost immediately after they were opened. Following extensive media coverage, large numbers of walkers took to the Wicklow Way and some of the boggier parts became badly overtrodden. Strategically important footbridges in Glencree and at the Watergates were swept away in floods, while loose waymark posts were either uprooted by vandals or accidentally run over by heavy forestry vehicles. The committees that helped to establish routes such as the South Leinster Way and Munster Way fell apart soon after blazing those trails, so that no-one was available to address maintenance issues. More seriously, problems concerning occupier's liability arose. Put simply, walkers injuring themselves in Ireland could, in theory, sue the landowner for damages. Disputes arose about who would cover the insurance costs for each of the trails and indemnify landowners against any potential claims for injuries. Given the complex nature of these problems, the development of the trail network ground to a halt for a couple of years.

Insurance, liability and maintenance issues were all addressed in the mid 1990s and new trails have since been blazed across the country to bring the Coast to Coast Walk to completion. The Wicklow Way and South Leinster Way continue to lead walkers onwards, as they always did. The Munster Way has been overhauled and is now known as the East Munster Way. The Avondhu Way and Duhallow Way are now promoted jointly as the Blackwater Way, and the Kerry Way remains a popular trail in the southwest. Together, these trails form the basis for the Irish Coast to Coast Walk. Apart from short gaps, almost the entire route is now waymarked and signposted. Walkers who leave the centre of Dublin and follow these trails to Bray Head on Valentia Island will cover up to 623km (387 miles). As most of the trails have been routed across gentle countryside, often using minor roads and forest tracks, walkers can usually adopt a brisk pace and should be able to cover the route in three weeks if they are used to walking long distances. This guide offers walkers information about the course of the Coast to Coast Walk, and the facilities available along the way.

The first edition of this guidebook was published in 1996, and its contents have since been completely overhauled. All the trails have been walked again and route alterations have been noted. Changes in the provision of facilities along the way – food, drink and accommodation – have also been checked. This edition also contains information on Ordnance Survey of Ireland Discovery Series maps (1:50,000), many of which were

COAST TO COAST GEOLOGY

The Skelligs seen from Bray Head on the Atlantic coast of Co Kerry (Day 24)

unavailable for the first edition. The diagrammatic maps presented in this guide illustrate the route and the main features you will pass on your way, but need to be used in association with the relevant OSI Discovery maps.

COAST TO COAST GEOLOGY

Coast to Coast walkers travel quickly from the urban sprawl of Dublin into some of the toughest terrain in the first few days of the journey. The Wicklow Mountains, Blackstairs Mountains and Brandon Hill are all part of a vast intrusion of granite that takes over a week to walk across! The course of the Wicklow Way meanders between the granite massif and the glistening schistose rock that surrounds it. The schist was formed when the molten mass of granite was intruded into the existing ancient Ordovician bedrock, altering the rock through a process of tremendous heat and pressure known as metamorphism. Kippure, Mullaghcleevaun and Tonelagee are granite, while Djouce and Croaghanmoira are schist. Lugnaquillia is unusual, because it is mostly granite, but has retained its original 'roof' of schist. On the whole, the granite uplands form vast, rounded, whaleback hills, while the schist tends to weather into more shapely peaks and has been excavated by glaciers, leaving deep glens between the mountains.

After passing Graiguenamanagh, the landscape of the South Leinster Way is dominated by the Three Sisters, the rivers Barrow, Nore and Suir. All three rivers seem to chart curious courses and appear to carve their way through entire ranges of hills and mountains. Opinions are divided as to whether these rivers have been 'super-

THE IRISH COAST TO COAST WALK

The busy thoroughfare of O'Connell Bridge in the heart of Dublin (Day 1)

imposed' on the landscape after wearing down through long-vanished upper layers of rock, or whether they display 'antecedent drainage' and have simply kept to their original courses despite any uplifting of the rock succession through geological time.

The Comeragh Mountains and Knockmealdown Mountains are formed of Old Red Sandstone; vast thicknesses of Devonian sands and grits that have been crumpled and contorted by immense pressures through the ages to produce this sandstone. In fact, this rock type is crossed by the East Munster Way, Blackwater Way and Kerry Way. Of particular interest is a feature known as the Armorican Front, the line dividing the predominantly Old Red Sandstone massif from the predominantly Carboniferous Limestone of the lowlands. You can look along this line and see the division clearly between the Knockmealdown Mountains and the River Suir, between the Nagles Mountains and the River Blackwater, and between the Derrynasaggart Mountains and the lowlands around Millstreet, Rathmore and Barraduff. Walkers are seldom aware of the Carboniferous Limestone. It dominates much of the Irish Midlands, but the Coast to Coast route steers clear of classic limestone features such as Mitchelstown Cave and Crag Cave. However, an exploration of the shores of Lough Leane or Muckross Lake in the Killarney National Park reveals water-worn limestone at its very best.

All the mountain groups crossed on the Irish Coast to Coast Walk feature typical corrie lakes and 'U' shaped glacial valleys. In the mountains of Co Kerry these are particularly well developed. The Kerry Way runs through the glacial Black Valley, and ice-scoured corries can be seen along the flanks of MacGillycuddy's Reeks and other mountain ranges. Only rarely do winter conditions remind walkers of the last Ice Age, as snow and ice seldom lie long on the Kerry mountains and are quickly removed by the warm, damp Atlantic airflows.

IRISH WEATHER

Ireland's proximity to the Atlantic Ocean guarantees that an almost constant westerly airflow brings warm, damp air over the country. Between 150 and 200 depressions track generally north of Ireland each year, so that frontal systems sweep regularly across the countryside. Each system is likely to bring rain, but there will generally be clear spells in between when the countryside shows off vibrant colours. As a general rule of thumb assume that March, April and May will be fairly dry and clear, though you may catch the tail-end of winter in the hills. In June, July and August expect showers, or even thunderstorms with the increasing heat and humidity. Flies can become a nuisance in these conditions and some insect repellent may need to be used. There is

THE IRISH COAST TO COAST WALK

sometimes the possibility of good walking weather around September and October, though the clear, cool, dry spells may be short-lived. The winter months are characterised by a drop in temperature, more rain and a possibility of some snow or sharp frosts. However, due to the oceanic influences, summers and winters in Ireland are not as markedly different as they are in Britain, or deep within Europe, where extremes are more likely. In Ireland, a week of sunny weather might be classed as a heat-wave, but it soon gives rise to a thick heat-haze that dulls the colours of the countryside. Snow can sometimes fall to some depth, but it seldom lasts long, except for small pockets in hollows in the hills.

Overall, you should expect all sorts of weather conditions to arrive in an apparently haphazard manner. Even on a simple day-walk you could experience striking variations. You need to pack waterproofs and you will certainly need to wear them at some point on the Irish Coast to Coast Walk. Take care when the sun shines as the pollution-free air can be clear, and cool breezes cover up the fact that you may be getting sunburnt. Pack sunscreen and use it. Rain in the hills is often accompanied by low cloud and mist, so be prepared to navigate using a map and compass. Although long-range weather forecasts are unlikely to be accurate, day-to-day forecasts are quite reliable. Try and tune into a radio, or catch a televised forecast in the evening, so that you can prepare yourself mentally and physically for the next day's weather conditions.

Take the time to study reminders of Ireland's ancient heritage along the trails

IRISH FLOWERS AND ANIMALS

Given the tremendous range of landscapes and habitats along the Coast to Coast Walk, any attempt to catalogue the species that might be noted along the way would degenerate into a mere list in the space available. However, you could pack a copy of the *Wicklow Way Natural History Field Guide*, by Ken Boyle and Orla Bourke, published by Cospoir. This gives an indication of the range of flora and fauna that was noted over twelve months on the northern stretch of the Wicklow Way. As the terrain on this stretch varies from forest to upland

IRISH FLOWERS AND ANIMALS

Sunlight playing on thin mist in a dense forestry plantation at Fiddane (Day 17)

moorlands and lowland glens, you would find similar terrain, and hence wildlife habitats, repeated across Ireland.

In general terms the uplands display open heathery slopes and blanket bogs, which often support patches of bilberry or wiry moor grass where the ground is reasonably dry. Sodden ground conditions allow bright green patches of sphagnum moss to form. Hares and foxes will run even to these heights, while grouse find cover in the heather. Ravens and other birds of prey may be seen wheeling overhead in search of smaller birds and mammals. Lonely pools of water serve to attract migrating wildfowl. As the uplands give way to the glens, heather gives way to invasive bracken and clumps of yellow-flowered, coconut-scented gorse. The more cultivated lowland glens and riversides may support a range of crops, but more likely it will be grassy pastures for sheep and cattle. Rabbits sometimes occur in great numbers in the lowlands, and the bird-life may be profuse. Although occasional stands of oak, ash, beech and alder may be passed, most trees outside the small woods and hedgerows will be commercial plantations of fast-growing spruces, pines and firs. When these trees are closely regimented, little light reaches the forest floor, which may simply be a sterile mat of dead needles. However, such plantations offer good cover to red deer and sika deer throughout the Wicklow Mountains, and both species are spreading further afield. They can

THE IRISH COAST TO COAST WALK

be spotted at dawn and dusk grazing along the grassy forest margins. Migrant birds, such as crossbills, have specially adapted beaks for teasing nuts from pine cones, and seskins also prefer coniferous forests.

Early summer is the best time to enjoy the bulk of the wild flowers, which bring a riot of colour to the hedgerows, riverbanks and roadside verges. Later in the summer, the heather flushes the hills with purple, while autumn tints change almost from day to day in deciduous woods and on bracken covered slopes. Autumn can be a good time for spotting migrant birds, while fungi may also be producing their strangely-shaped fruiting bodies.

While the *Wicklow Way Natural History Field Guide* will serve you well for most of the Irish Coast to Coast Walk, the Kerry countryside deserves a special mention as it is populated by species not found elsewhere in the country. Pure Irish red deer inhabit The Wilderness on the slopes of Mangerton Mountain, while the Kerry spotted slug is a curious creature often seen grazing after heavy rain. Floral tributes include species with a peculiar worldwide distribution, in that they occur naturally only in the south-west of Ireland and the Pyrenees, or around the Mediterranean. These include the saxifrage known as St Patrick's cabbage (or London pride), the arbutus (or strawberry tree), and the insectivorous blue- flowered greater butterwort.

In the winter months, by the Upper Lake in the Killarney National Park, a flock of white-fronted geese from Greenland may be grazing, and this may result in a diversion of the Kerry Way. Only towards the end of the Irish Coast to Coast Walk do seabirds really make an impression, but time spent on Valentia Island's Bray Head will reveal a host of species. A cruise out to the Skelligs will reveal gannet colonies and, in season, puffins.

ACCESS TO THE COUNTRYSIDE

The waymarked trails that make up the Irish Coast to Coast Walk have been pieced together from various

The waymarks prove useful on misty days on the upland parts of the route

ROUTE FINDING

paths, tracks and country roads. Whenever possible, the roads used are fairly quiet, narrow, minor roads. Paths and tracks through the countryside may be rights of way – over which foot travellers may freely pass – but in some instances access has been negotiated for walkers. Generally negotiated routes do not become rights of way, but the landowner grants a 'wayleave', which can be withdrawn at any time. Tracks through State forests are usually accessible at any time, but can be closed during harvesting operations.

The granting of a wayleave can involve certain conditions having to be fulfilled, such as a ban on camping or dogs. It is important that walkers following the waymarked trails behave considerably at all times and remember that the land they are crossing is someone else's livelihood. Don't take dogs across farmland or disturb livestock. Be sure to close gates and cross stiles carefully to avoid damaging fences. Don't pollute watercourses, light fires or leave litter. Camping is expressly forbidden in State forests and National Parks, but many landowners will permit a tent to be pitched in the corner of a field if approached with a polite request. The trails are not intended to be used by cyclists or horse riders, except where such use is already established. Nor are large groups or mass sponsored walks encouraged as heavy use over a short period can result in damage to fragile surfaces in some places.

Insurance cover has been provided for the waymarked trails; mainly to indemnify landowners from potential claims made against them by walkers injuring themselves. To be fair, your personal safety is really your own responsibility while you are walking through the countryside, and this forms the core of the Occupier's Liability Act of 1995.

ROUTE FINDING

The waymarks used on the Irish Coast to Coast Walk almost universally bear a 'walking man' symbol, which may appear on both waymark posts and roadside signposts. Generally, an arrow will show the intended direction as left, right or straight ahead. Some waymark posts may simply bear an arrow without the 'walking man' symbol. In some areas waymarking may be sparse, and at some crucial junctions a marker post or signpost may have gone missing, or been turned the wrong way, so keep an eye on the route description and maps. There are a couple of short gaps

Close the gate and respect the life and working traditions of the countryside

THE IRISH COAST TO COAST WALK

between some of the trails that have not been waymarked to date, so a suggested stretch of road-walking is included to make a quick and effective link. Look on the waymarks as confirming that you are still on course, and be suspicious if you haven't seen one for some time. Check the maps and guidebook to see if you are still on course. From time to time the trails do need to be altered and it is hoped that such alterations will be clearly marked when you reach them.

MAP COVERAGE

The entire course of the Irish Coast to Coast Walk is covered by Ordnance Survey of Ireland (OSI) Discovery Series mapping at a scale of 1:50,000. These are quite adequate for the walk and show good detail, and are particularly useful if you want to see the bigger picture, or if you want to make sweeping diversions through some of the nearby mountains. Individual sheet numbers are quoted throughout the guidebook. Most good bookshops carry a stock of OSI maps, as well as most Tourist Information Offices. Many Ordnance Survey map stockists in Britain carry some OSI sheets.

The sketch maps in this guidebook illustrate the route and major points of interest along the way and should be used in collaboration with the OSI maps. Fourteen Discovery sheets cover the route, namely 50, 56, 61, 62, 68, 70, 74, 75, 76, 78, 79, 80, 81 and 83. (Four of these maps cover only very short distances: 61, 70, 76 & 81.) There is a detailed OSI street map of Dublin that proves useful on the first day. Harveys produce a detailed 1:30,000 scale map of the Wicklow Mountains. There are

Routes seldom climb high in the mountains, but can cross rugged countryside

detailed 1:25,000 Ordnance Survey maps of Killarney National Park and MacGillycuddy's Reeks towards the end of the route (though the latter is out of print).

TRAVEL TO IRELAND

By Air: There are daily flights to Dublin Airport from many British airports (including the London airports, Bristol, Birmingham, Manchester, Glasgow and Edinburgh). Dozens of European airports have direct flights to Dublin (you can fly from France, Belgium, The Netherlands, Germany, Portugal, Spain, Italy, Austria, Switzerland, Scandinavia and parts of Eastern Europe). In the United States flights to Dublin operate from New York, Boston, Washington, Chicago and Los Angeles. Flights are almost always scheduled, rather than chartered. Ireland's national airline is Aer Lingus (**www.aerlingus.ie**) but Ryanair (**www.ryanair.com**) runs just as many services. Aer Arann also fly some useful routes between British and Irish airports (**www.aerarann.com**). Budget flights to Ireland are probably best checked and booked on the internet, as many travel agents are loathe to deal with bookings where profits are tiny. The Irish Coast to Coast Walk starts in the middle of Dublin, which is only a few minutes travel time from the airport. Fast and frequent express buses run between the airport and Dublin's main bus and rail stations. Alight on O'Connell Street and you can start the walk! There is the option, on completing the Coast to Coast Walk, of flying out of Kerry Airport to Dublin or London, rather than travelling all the way across country by road or rail.

By Ferry: Fast ferries to Dublin and Dun Laoghaire operate from Holyhead in North Wales, berthing not far from the start of the Irish Coast to Coast Walk. There are other ferries from South Wales to Rosslare Harbour, though this leaves onward journeys by train or bus to Dublin. Other possible ferry routes include those from Liverpool to Dublin, Swansea to Cork, Roscoff to Cork, Cherbourg to Rosslare Harbour, as well as ferries from Scotland to Northern Ireland. The major operator on the Irish Sea routes is Irish Ferries (**www.irishferries.com**).

By Train: It is possible to buy train tickets in Britain and other countries around Europe that include travel on one of the ferry services, as well as onward rail travel across Ireland. Enquire at the main staffed railway stations for timetable information and tickets to choose a journey at an acceptable price (**www.irishrail.ie**).

By Coach: Express Eurolines' coaches operate over a comprehensive network that links Dublin with 1500 places in Britain; plus 280 major European towns and cities in more than 20 countries. Obviously, if travelling the length of Europe using coach services, possibly with a number of

THE IRISH COAST TO COAST WALK

connections, you could be on the road a long time (**www.eurolines.ie**).

GETTING AROUND IRELAND

By Train: Rail services in Ireland fan outwards from Dublin. If you wish to split the Irish Coast to Coast Walk by breaking at a town with a railway station, then Carrick-on-Suir and Clonmel fall at approximately the half-way stage. Other places with railway stations include Mallow, Millstreet and Killarney. Once the Coast to Coast Walk is completed, rail services can be used from Killarney to return to Dublin (**www.irishrail.ie**).

By Bus: The national bus network is operated by Bus Eireann, and although services are sparse in the early stages of the Coast to Coast Walk, many towns and villages are better served later. St Kevin's Bus runs daily from Dublin to Glendalough. Bus Eireann serves Tinahely only a couple of days a week, though daily services are available at Bunclody, close to where the Wicklow Way and South Leinster Way meet. Carrick-on-Suir and Clonmel have plenty of bus services and both places are on the East Munster Way. Fermoy, on the Blackwater Way, is equally well served. After a stretch with infrequent bus services, there are better connections around Millstreet and Killarney. Make note of the bus services beyond Killarney, on the way to Cahersiveen, as these will be needed at the end of the long walk across Ireland (**www.buseireann.ie**).

ACCOMMODATION

There is a basic accommodation list at the end of this guidebook. It covers hostels, bed and breakfast, guesthouses and hotels that occur on or fairly close to the Coast to Coast Walk. If they are significantly off-route this is noted, and you may wish to ask if a pick-up and drop-off can be arranged. The list is a basic contact list only, and does not include details of prices or facilities, so be sure to check those things when you first make enquiries. The main purpose of the list is to alert walkers to the range of accommodation on or near the route, so that you don't need to search

Extensive use is made of forest tracks and quiet country roads

ACCOMMODATION

through long listings to try and find the few addresses you actually need.

Backpacking: There are very few organised campsites along the route, but some hostels and a few country bed and breakfast places will allow an informal pitch. In some cases, farmers may also allow an informal pitch if approached politely beforehand. Expect farmers to be indignant if they find you have pitched in their fields without asking permission!

Hostelling: There are a few *An Oige* Youth Hostels and a few independent hostels along the course of the Coast to Coast Walk. Although there aren't nearly enough hostels along the route for walkers to stay in one every night, they can be supplemented with nights in bed and breakfast places, so that the route can be walked within a fairly low budget.

Bed and Breakfast: There are plenty of cosy bed and breakfast places along the Coast to Coast Walk. They may be town houses or farmhouses, often inhabited by families who make you feel welcome and who can speak volumes about their own localities. If you want to move upmarket, there are more luxurious guest houses and hotels along the way. All generally serve a 'full Irish breakfast' in the mornings which will set most walkers up for the day. If packed lunches or evening meals are required, it is always best to enquire well in advance. If an establishment is off-route, proprietors may be willing to pick you up from the route and drop you off the next day, but again it is best to enquire in advance if this is possible.

Block Bookings: Some walkers like the security of having all their

B&Bs are quite plentiful in some areas but are totally absent in other areas

THE IRISH COAST TO COAST WALK

B&Bs off route, such as Park Lodge (Day 6), may offer pick-ups by arrangement

accommodation arranged in advance. This is fine, but it leaves them tied to a rigid schedule that can prove impossible to alter. If bad weather or fatigue brings progress to a slow crawl or even a halt, it can be a nightmare trying to unwind a carefully-planned schedule. There would be no option but to skip a day's walk and the continuity of the route would be broken. Some walking holiday companies provide accommodation packages for popular waymarked trails, such as the Wicklow Way and Kerry Way, but none of them yet offer a complete Coast to Coast package.

Book a Bed Ahead: Some of the larger Tourist Information Offices in Ireland operate an advance booking system. Pop into one of these places and they will be able to phone around and secure you a booking almost anywhere. However, these larger offices are invariably off the Coast to Coast Walk. There is a handy freephone service that you could use while travelling, enabling you to make a booking and pay by credit card (tel 00800 66866866).

Warning: When you make an accommodation booking, you are entering into an agreement with the proprietor. They may ask for a deposit, or your credit card details. If you fail to turn up, or cancel too late, they may not be able to re-allocate your bed and therefore be entitled to some recompense. If you fail to reach a destination where you have made a booking, contact the proprietor and explain. In some instances, when walkers fail to show, the emergency services might be contacted, and could be searching needlessly for you while you are safely tucked up in bed elsewhere!

FOOD AND DRINK

Ireland is famous for its pubs, though on some parts of the Coast to Coast Walk they may be in short supply. In fact, there are many days when there is simply no point of refreshment along the route. A typical Irish country pub may have a limited stock of drink and no food at all, but if they are on the route and offer a brief respite from inclement weather, walkers are unlikely to complain. Some of the more popular pubs offer a great choice of food and drink. They may provide traditional wholesome Irish meals such as 'bacon 'n' cabbage', while more upmarket places may specialise in seafood and a surprisingly international cuisine.

MONEY

Ireland uses the Euro, which is available in notes valued at 500, 100, 50, 20, 10 and 5 Euro. Coins are valued at 2 and 1 Euro, with loose change coming as 50, 20, 10, 5, 2 and 1 cents. Banks with ATMs are available around Dublin and in the larger towns along the way, so you may have to carry a large amount of cash for several days. Some hotels, guest

THE IRISH COAST TO COAST WALK

Country pubs are a welcome sight on the Coast to Coast Walk, but they may be off-route

houses and larger restaurants accept credit cards or cheques, but most bed and breakfast establishments and small pubs deal only in cash. Towns with banks and ATMs are noted along the Coast to Coast Walk. Make sure you carry enough cash so that you don't have to make unnecessary detours off-route.

TOURIST INFORMATION OFFICES

Dublin and the larger towns along the Coast to Coast Walk have Tourist Information Offices. They can help with accommodation bookings and will have full details about local services and attractions. Maps, guidebooks and souvenirs may be on sale. Many villages along the way may have a small Tourist Information Point, which may be part of a small shop where little more than a stock of leaflets are dispensed, or it may simply be a notice board listing local information.

WHEN TO WALK

The Irish Coast to Coast Walk can be attempted at almost any time of year, but in the winter months there can be problems. Snow falls only rarely in Ireland, but it does tend to lie longest and deepest in the Wicklow Mountains. Sometimes, it can rain for weeks in the winter and the ground can become very soft, wet and muddy. Indeed, it can be wet almost any time of the year, but the spring

Shops, banks, post offices, pubs and restaurants along the way are mentioned

months can be refreshingly cool and clear. May can be an excellent month. Summer may bring a short-lived heatwave, but it may well be followed by a storm and unsettled weather. Autumn sometimes throws up a surprise and the month of October can be reasonably dry. In Ireland, you will find that the weather varies not only from day to day, but it can vary wildly throughout the day. Expect to be caught in the rain at some point, and expect mist on high ground from time to time. Lightweight waterproofs will be sufficient for a Coast to Coast Walk in the summer months.

THE IRISH COAST TO COAST WALK

Religious grottos, shrines, holy wells and pilgrimage sites are encountered

Footwear should include lightweight boots for wet and muddy ground, but consider lightweight trainers or shock-absorbing innersoles for some of the road-walks and hard forest tracks.

ONE MAN AND HIS DOG

It has always been possible to take dogs between Britain and Ireland with a minimum of fuss. It is now possible to bring dogs from other parts of Europe provided they are inoculated and come with the appropriate paperwork. However, think twice before taking your dog along any of the waymarked trails described in this guidebook. Dogs are frequently seen as a menace by Irish farmers, and as the trails have often been negotiated as wayleaves where they cross farmland, it may be that the landowner expressly forbids entry to dogs.

DAILY SCHEDULE

If you have a clear idea of your usual walking pace through different types of countryside, then you will have no problem working out a comfortable daily schedule. The Irish Coast to Coast Walk uses minor roads, forest tracks, bog roads, open hillsides and occasional riverside or field paths. The terrain is mostly gentle, but can be demanding. The 24-day schedule offered in this guidebook is built around the availability of accommodation, food and drink. It means that some days are long and others are short, the average being 26km (16 miles) per day. There may be an opportunity to cut a long day into two

Walkers lean into the steep, heathery slope to climb Knockmealdown following a high-level alternative to Days 13 and 14

shorter sections, or it may be possible to extend a short day's walk to the next place with suitable accommodation. Some walkers would be able to complete the Irish Coast to Coast Walk in three weeks or less, while others would prefer four weeks. The whole route can be split into two stretches of a fortnight each or four stretches of a week apiece, including travel to and from each stage. Walkers who live in Ireland can consider a series of weekend or one-day walks to extend the pleasure of the trip over a whole year or more!

EMERGENCY SERVICES

In Ireland you can dial either 999 or 112 to alert the emergency services. The gardaí (police), ambulance, fire service, coastguard and mountain rescue can be contacted this way. Be ready to give full details of any emergency, and either stay by the phone, or give them your phone number so that they can stay in contact with you.

STAGE 1
The Wicklow Way

Gorse bushes on the slopes of Garryhoe frame a view of Croaghanmoira (Day 5)

DAY 1
Dublin to Marlay Park

Start	O'Connell Bridge, Dublin (grid ref 160343)
Finish	Marlay Park (grid ref 155267)
Distance	11km (7 miles)
Cumulative Distance	11km (7 miles)
Maps	OSI Discovery 50, OSI Dublin Street Map
Terrain	Busy city streets and occasional parks
Refreshments	Plenty of shops, bars and restaurants throughout the city. There are tearooms at Rathfarnham Castle, St Enda's Park and Marlay Park.

The Irish Coast to Coast Walk starts on Dublin's busiest thoroughfare where the tidal River Liffey slips under O'Connell Bridge. This first day's walk, or half-day's walk, is mostly along busy city streets, so wear comfortable footwear. There are a few fine parks along the way where you can take a break from the bustle in a pleasant green space and maybe enjoy a picnic. Feel free to vary the route if you wish to visit any particular shops, pubs or museums in the city. The aim for this first day is to reach Marlay Park on the southern outskirts of Dublin, where the waymarked Wicklow Way begins.

Pause for a moment on **O'Connell Bridge** to consider your long walk across Ireland. It may be difficult to think ahead while traffic rumbles all around and people surge past in great haste! Purists might feel obliged to start by dipping their feet in the waters of the River Liffey and this can be done, with great care, by descending slippery steps on Aston Quay, beside O'Connell Bridge. Once this ritual has been performed, then the long walk can commence across country to the Kerry coast. A word of warning at the start; please take great care crossing busy roads throughout the day.

THE WICKLOW WAY: DAY 1 – DUBLIN TO MARLAY PARK

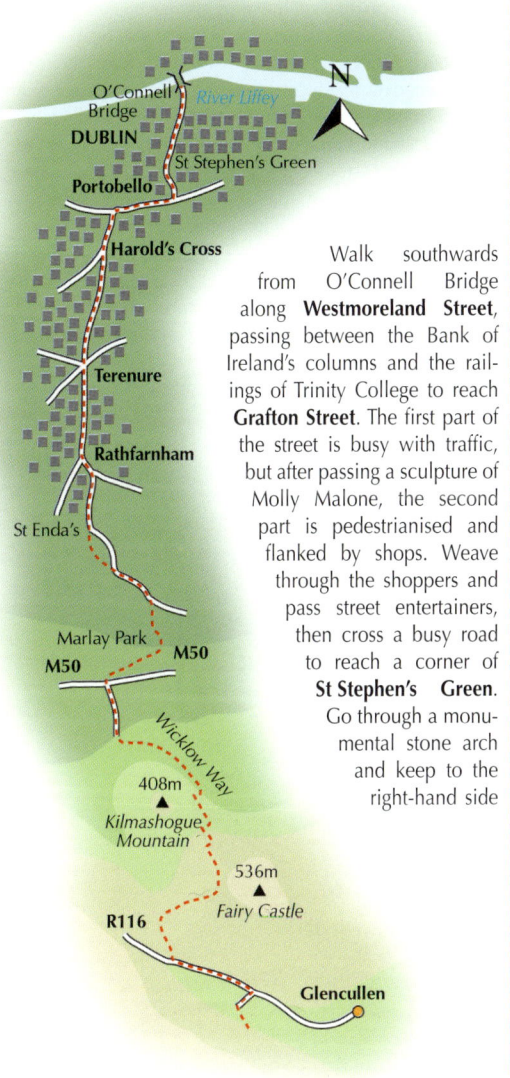

Walk southwards from O'Connell Bridge along **Westmoreland Street**, passing between the Bank of Ireland's columns and the railings of Trinity College to reach **Grafton Street**. The first part of the street is busy with traffic, but after passing a sculpture of Molly Malone, the second part is pedestrianised and flanked by shops. Weave through the shoppers and pass street entertainers, then cross a busy road to reach a corner of **St Stephen's Green**. Go through a monumental stone arch and keep to the right-hand side

THE IRISH COAST TO COAST WALK

of the park to exit at the next corner gateway. Cross another busy road and the LUAS railway, then walk along **Harcourt Street**, admiring its Georgian houses. Accommodation is available along here. Turn right and left to continue along **Charlemont Street**. Don't cross over the **Grand Canal** at the Barge Bar, but turn right to follow a quiet path alongside it.

Cross over a busy road at the next bridge, which is at **Portobello**, and continue alongside the canal from a lock. Signposts point to the right, first for The Shaw Birthplace, then for the Irish Jewish Museum, if detours can be considered. A row of cosy one-storey cottages run along **Portobello Road**. Turn left to cross the next busy

Daniel O'Connell, 'The Liberator', looks down at you in Dublin at the start of the walk

THE WICKLOW WAY: DAY 1 – DUBLIN TO MARLAY PARK

road bridge and walk straight along **Harold's Cross Road**. Keep to the left of a small triangular park full of tall trees and flower beds, flanked by busy roads. Pass Harold's Cross Greyhound Stadium, and later continue along **Terenure Road North** and **Rathfarnham Road**, eventually crossing the River Dodder. Terenure and Rathfarnham are both villages that have been swallowed by Dublin's urban sprawl. Pass **Rathfarnham Castle** or, if there is time, include a visit.

Continue round to the left along **Grange Road**, which itself turns right and is signposted for St Enda's Park and Marlay Park. Note the Loreto Abbey on the left, with its impressive gateway. Turn right along **Sarah Curran Avenue** and enter **St Enda's National Historic Park**. Take any route using any path, but head for the house which is also the Pearse Museum. There is a tearoom and toilets,

The Pearse Museum can be visited at the end of the day in St Enda's Park

THE IRISH COAST TO COAST WALK

as well as a rather apt poem by Padraig Pearse entitled *The Wayfarer*. Exit from the park near a road junction and turn left towards the Eden Lounge Bar and restaurant. Along the road, use one of two gateways on the right to enter **Marlay Park**; if it has closed for the evening catch a bus back into Dublin and head for your accommodation. Dublin Bus 47B runs regularly between Hawkins Street in the middle of Dublin and Marlay Park on the southern outskirts of the city.

DUBLIN'S FAIR CITY

Dublin is the biggest city in Ireland, so it naturally boasts a full range of facilities. Accommodation ranges from simple hostels to splendid hotels. Banks usually have ATMs. There are post offices, shops of every description, including outdoor-gear stores. Toilets are located around the city centre and in the parks. There are abundant pubs and restaurants, offering everything from traditional Irish food and drink to every international taste imaginable. As the transport hub of Ireland, there are buses and trains fanning out to all parts of the country. Dublin Bus runs a comprehensive service around the city and a light rail system known as the LUAS is also in operation. A tourist information office on Suffolk Street, off Grafton Street, can advise about all the attractions of the city (tel 01–6057700).

If you want to make a thorough exploration of Dublin, then you will need to allow at least a week for it before you even think about the Coast to Coast Walk. The city was founded on the River Liffey over a 1000 years ago by the Vikings, so there is plenty of accumulated history. However, if you are only interested in brief notes about points of interest along the way, then a few minutes at each of the following places shouldn't cause undue delay.

O'Connell Bridge

O'Connell Bridge was named after Daniel O'Connell, whose monument is on the north side of the River Liffey. He was born in 1775 and became a distinguished and active barrister and politician. He formed the Catholic Association in 1823, which became a popular and influential movement. Guided by O'Connell, the association was a driving force leading to the Catholic Emancipation of 1829. He was instrumental in moves to repeal the Act of Union of 1800 and earned the title of The Liberator. O'Connell's fine

THE WICKLOW WAY: DAY 1 – DUBLIN TO MARLAY PARK

monument is flanked by four angels symbolising Eloquence, Courage, Fidelity and Patriotism. Holes in their wings were caused by flying bullets during the Easter Rising of 1916, which left Dublin's city centre in ruins.

Westmoreland Street
If you can pause for a moment without obstructing the crowds, then look up from shop level and marvel at the varied architecture of the upper stories of the buildings. Styles include Italian, Dutch and French which are set side-by-side. Note the old façade that has been incorporated into the glass frontage of the Educational Building Society. Across the road is Bewley's, where you might consider a break for tea or coffee before walking across Ireland. Apparently, you haven't *been* to Dublin if you haven't been to Bewley's!

Bank of Ireland
The building with the striking circular walls supported on all sides by columns was originally the House of Parliament but has been used by the Bank of Ireland since the Act of Union of 1800. It can be entered via impressive porticos and there can be no finer place to conduct a financial transaction as under the chandelier near the blazing fire. Bureau de change facilities are available for visiting walkers who still need a pocketful of Euros. The former House of Lords still retains much of its original form and that part of the building can be visited at certain times.

Trinity College
Trinity College was founded by Queen Elizabeth I in 1592. An exploration would take all day, but you could at least walk through the gateway and tread the 'hallowed cobbles', passing from the bustling city streets into an oasis of industrious calm. The famous *Book of Kells* is located in the Old Library and one of its lavishly illuminated pages is turned each day to be viewed by a long line of visitors. The college is entitled, under the Copyright Act, to one copy of every book published in the British Isles; including this one. There is an audio-visual exhibition about the College, if you can spare the time for it.

Molly Malone
A sculpture of Molly Malone, complete with wheelbarrow, cockles and mussels 'alive alive-o' stands halfway along Grafton Street between the slow-moving traffic and the pedestrianised section. Molly is often surrounded by

THE IRISH COAST TO COAST WALK

The arched entry to Trinity College is passed shortly after starting the walk

street artists, who give way to buskers and entire musical ensembles as you continue along the street. Jugglers and magicians may also be spotted, as well as eloquent street poets, before you reach St Stephen's Green.

St Stephen's Green
This is a large rectangular park in the care of Dúchas (the Heritage Service). In fact, their office overlooks the green and they have responsibility for property all over Ireland. St Stephen's Green was enclosed in the late 17th

century, but it wasn't landscaped until 1877. This was done with the support of Lord Ardilaun, or Arthur Guinness (brewer of the 'black stuff '). The green is richly ornamental and is well used by residents and visitors to Dublin for rest and enjoyment. If you arrive too early in the day, the gates may be closed, but you can still walk alongside the railings.

The Grand Canal
The Grand Canal runs from Dublin's Ringsend Basin to the mighty River Shannon at Shannon Harbour in Co Offaly. There is a continuous towpath, which is fully waymarked for walkers beyond the city sprawl, offering a splendid and easy low-level cross-country walk of around 80 miles (130km). The stretch at Portobello was constructed in 1790. **Note:** The Grand Canal can be used to provide an alternative low-level start to the Coast to Coast Walk. The Grand Canal towpath, with the Barrow Line and River Barrow towpath, can be followed from Dublin to Graiguenamanagh on the South Leinster Way.

Rathfarnham Castle
This castle has a rather plain exterior, being essentially a fortified dwelling. It was in continuous occupation from 1585 to 1985. The first occupant was its builder, a Yorkshire clergyman named Adam Loftus, who became Archbishop of Dublin and Chancellor of Ireland. After changing hands many times, it was held by the Society of Jesus, who sold it to the State. After careful restoration, Rathfarnham Castle has been opened to the public, though the interior is still being developed. The castle has a small tearoom and toilets.

St Enda's National Historic Park
St Enda's School was founded by Padraig Pearse and opened in 1908. Lessons were taught through the medium of Irish, but the school suffered financial problems. Pearse was involved in the nationalist struggle and allowed the house and grounds to be used for covert military activities. It was Pearse who read out the *Declaration of the Republic* from the steps of the General Post Office on O'Connell Street, an act which was to lead to his execution shortly afterwards at Kilmainham Jail. St Enda's houses some of Pearse's effects and the whole park is managed by Dúchas. Remember to get through the park before it closes at dusk, and to check opening times if the house is to be visited.

The Irish Coast to Coast Walk

DAY 2
Marlay Park to Knockree

Start	Marlay Park (grid ref 155267)
Finish	Knockree Youth Hostel (grid ref 192151)
Distance	20km (12.5 miles)
Cumulative Distance	31km (19.5 miles)
Maps	OSI Discovery 50 & 56, Harvey Maps' *Wicklow Mountains*
Terrain	Easy paths, tracks and roads at the start. Forest tracks and boggy moorland paths are broken by stretches of road-walking.
Refreshments	Marlay Park has a coffee house. Johnnie Fox's Pub is off-route in Glencullen. Enniskerry, also off-route, has pubs and restaurants.

The Wicklow Way is probably the busiest of Ireland's waymarked trails, being on the doorstep of Dublin and easily accessible to all its inhabitants. However, it can also be very quiet at times and you may be the only person following it. The route leaves Marlay Park and crosses the Dublin Mountains to reach the higher Wicklow Mountains beyond. Bear in mind that facilities are mostly off-route and accommodation is sparse. Carry extra supplies and book at least a couple of nights' accommodation in advance. While most of the route is along minor roads and forest tracks, there are some upland stretches that can be muddy in wet weather.

The Wicklow Way actually starts in a car park near **Marlay House** where there is a large sign full of park notices, as well as a sketch map of the route as far as Luggala. Turn left on leaving the car park to spot the first Wicklow Way marker post; a yellow arrow and 'walking man' indicate a right turn. Walk into a wooded area and turn right, then later turn left over a bridge with a view of a **pond**. Turn right at a sculpture of the *Four Seasons* then

MARLAY PARK

Marlay Park opens at 10am each morning and can be reached from Dublin using Dublin Bus 47B. Arrive too early and you will either have to wait for the gates to open or walk around the boundary wall by road. Spare the time to explore a little before setting off, but don't leave too late. There are craft workshops around a courtyard, as well as the Courtyard Coffee Shop and nearby toilets. The Regency Walled Garden is worth visiting too. Marlay House, centrepiece of the park, was built at the end of the 18th century, but rebuilt in the 19th century.

---

enjoy another view of the pond from a special stance. Turn right and left and follow the woodland path to the southern edge of the park. Turn right along a tarmac path parallel to the **Southern Cross Route Motorway**. Leave the park at a car park and turn right, still walking parallel to the motorway. Turn left under the motorway, then left again up **Kilmashogue Lane**. Pass the ruins of an old mill and a number of expensive properties as the road climbs uphill and leaves Dublin behind.

Turn left at a 'Coillte' sign for **Kilmashogue**, where there is a car park and abundant notices forbidding parking

Marlay Park, on the outskirts of Dublin, is where the Wicklow Way begins

THE IRISH COAST TO COAST WALK

A waymark post outside Kilmashogue Woods on the slopes of Fairy Castle

anywhere else. There are essentially three tracks ahead on the forested slope, so take the middle one as marked. The track is gritty and climbs alongside a **golf course**, with views back over Dublin's urban sprawl. The track appears to be heading for a series of communication masts on Three Rock Mountain, but there is a zig-zag up into denser forest and the masts pass from sight. Views over Dublin and Dublin Bay may also stretch far beyond to the distant Mountains of Mourne. The masts are seen again, but turn right to leave the track and follow a steep, bouldery and well-worn path up the forested slope. The waymarked trail turns right to reach the edge of the forest, then turns left uphill alongside the forest, but there is a short-cut straight to the edge of the forest.

The path is aligned to a boundary ditch and fence as it climbs uphill. At the top of the moorland crest, at around 490m (1600ft) on the shoulder of **Fairy Castle**, turn right and head gradually downhill, still walking alongside a boundary ditch and fence. Approaching a forest on **Tibradden Mountain**, turn left and follow another clear path downhill alongside the trees. Go through a little gate and the path swings right among the trees, dropping to the R116 road at **Ballybrack**. Take care when landing on this road as traffic is difficult to spot, then turn left and pass the **Pine Forest Art Centre** and a few small farms. Further along the road there is a turning space for Dublin Bus 44B, an occasional service linking Dublin and **Glencullen**. ◄

The road, incidentally, can be followed to a crossroads at Glencullen, where Johnnie Fox's Pub, founded in 1798, claims to be the highest pub in Ireland!

Turn sharp right down Boranaraltry Lane and cross **Boranaraltry Bridge** over Glencullen River. Head onwards and upwards across the valley side, passing through a gate at a point where a stream crosses the track. Climb higher along an open stretch of track and go through another gate. Keep walking until you can turn right up another track. This wriggles up a slope of young forest, so there are still views of the valley as well

40

The Wicklow Way: Day 2 – Marlay Park to Knockree

as a good stretch of the Irish Sea beyond Killiney. At a junction of tracks keep straight on as marked, and as height is gained, look back to see if the Mountains of Mourne can be spotted far beyond Dublin Bay. The Isle of Man and North Wales might also be seen in exceptionally clear weather. At the top end of the forest, the track moves out at around 470m (1540ft) onto the moorland slopes of **Prince William's Seat**, and the conical form of the Great Sugar Loaf can often be seen, as well as a good stretch of coast. The route passes from Co Dublin to Co Wicklow at this point.

The waymarked course follows a boggy, over-trodden path a little way down from the track, though coming in the other direction the track is the route waymarked. Either way, follow the track and walk onwards to reach a junction of tracks at **Ravens Rock**. At this point, follow a path marked diagonally to the right across a slope of heather and bilberry, heading towards a forest. Walk down between the trees, watching for boulders and exposed roots, as well as marker posts, to land on a track. Follow the bendy track down to a parking space beside the road at **Curtlestown Wood**.

Turn right along the road, then left at a road junction, as signposted for the Wicklow Way and Glendalough. Walk up and down the narrow road, then turn left up a forest track, passing a barrier on the slopes of **Knockree**. The track levels out, with a fine view of the Great Sugar Loaf, then a grassy path heads off to the right. Turn right again to follow a steeper path down to another road in **Glencree**. At this point, the

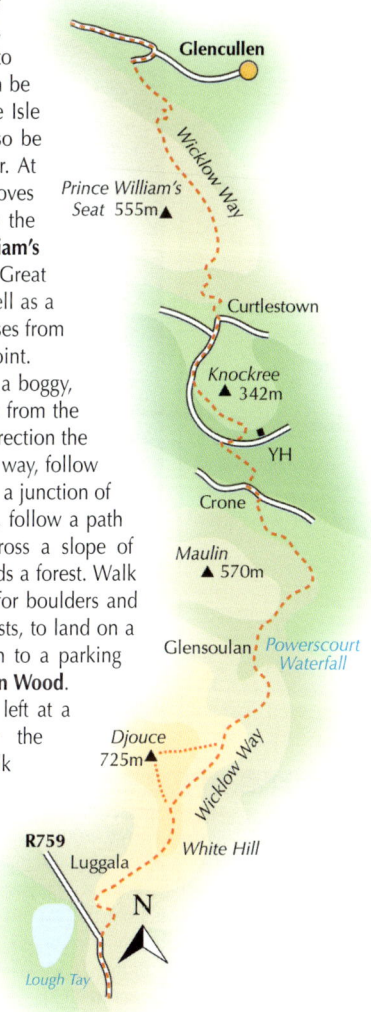

41

THE IRISH COAST TO COAST WALK

A view of the prominent peak of Great Sugar Loaf from the route in Glencree

Wicklow Way continues across the road, heading down to the right, but walkers who are aiming for **Knockree Youth Hostel** or Enniskerry will turn left along the road. The hostel is just along the road in a huddle of whitewashed former farm buildings. Hostellers should carry supplies with them as the hostel does not normally sell food, and shops in the village of Enniskerry are well off-route.

ENNISKERRY

This little village is clustered around an attractive square and although 3km (2 miles) off-route, it offers a good range of facilities. There are a couple of hotels and B&Bs in the area; with a B&B at Glaskenny being closest to the Wicklow Way, not far from the youth hostel. There are shops and a post office, as well as pubs and restaurants. Dublin Bus 44 links Dublin with Enniskerry, while Dublin Bus 185 links Bray with Enniskerry and the Shop River, running a little closer to Glaskenny and the youth hostel.

DAY 3
Knockree to Laragh

Start	Knockree Youth Hostel (grid ref 192151)
Finish	Laragh (grid ref 143966)
Distance	28km (17 miles)
Cumulative Distance	59km (36.5 miles)
Maps	OSI Discovery 56, Harvey Maps' *Wicklow Mountains*
Terrain	Riverside and forest tracks give way to paths across open moorland slopes. More forest tracks are followed by road walking and easy hill paths.
Refreshments	Roundwood is off-route and has a few pubs and restaurants. Laragh has a few more pubs and restaurants.

Today's walk includes some of the best mountain scenery along the Wicklow Way, along with an option to climb to the summit of Djouce if you aspire to higher things. However, it is also a long day's walk, bearing in mind the ascents and descents along the way, and some walkers would be happy to move off-route to Roundwood and cover the distance over two days at a more leisurely pace. The Wicklow Way used to be routed through the village of Laragh, but now by-passes it by a short distance. The village has a full range of facilities and no doubt many walkers continue to visit the place in search of accommodation, food and drink.

If you start the day from **Knockree Youth Hostel** you can short-cut by simply crossing the road, crossing a stile and walking down into the valley to join the Wicklow Way. To stick faithfully to the route, however, leave the hostel and turn right along the road, then head down to the left as signposted for the Wicklow Way. Walk down a narrow forest track from a barrier, and take the second turning on the left as marked. Walk along a narrow path and cross a stile before dropping down to the **Glencree River**. Turn

THE IRISH COAST TO COAST WALK

Close up to the powerful Powerscourt Waterfall in the Wicklow Mountains

THE WICKLOW WAY: DAY 3 – KNOCKREE TO LARAGH

left to follow it downstream, passing pools used for swimming and grassy patches used as unofficial campsites. A **footbridge** is reached on a bend in the river.

Cross over the footbridge and keep right to follow a path and forest track up to a road. Turn left along the road to **Crone House**, bearing in mind that nearby Coolakay House offers food and accommodation in the valley. Turn right up through a car park as signposted for the Wicklow Way and Glendalough. Follow a track uphill from the far end of the car park and turn left at a junction. Keep climbing along the track as marked, and it eventually levels out above **Bahana**. A couple of zig-zag bends take the track up to a splendid viewpoint around 300m (985ft) at Ride Rock. **Powerscourt Waterfall** plunges into a deep, forested glen, with the rounded shape of Djouce rising beyond. The Great Sugar Loaf is also in view.

POWERSCOURT

The 18th-century mansion of Powerscourt House and its beautiful ornamental gardens are well off the course of the Wicklow Way. Powerscourt Deerpark, however, can be viewed from the lofty stance of the Ride Rock. The main attraction is Powerscourt Waterfall, which slides vigorously down slabs of granite and presents a powerful spectacle after heavy rain. The surrounding woodlands were planted on bare ground a century ago, and while the deer park is now defunct, descendents of its former inhabitants may still be seen in the locality. Red deer and sika deer have interbred so that red/sika hybrids might give rise to confusion when first spotted.

Keep to the track to leave **Ride Rock**, rising across a steep slope of heather, bracken and bilberry. It becomes a narrow path across a more wooded slope, passing an outcrop of schist before heading into denser forest. Watch carefully for the marked path, as well as for boulders and exposed tree roots. When the path reaches the edge of the forest at 380m (1250ft), turn left and walk down to a footbridge spanning the **River Dargle** at the Watergates. This is another popular unofficial campsite.

Walk straight uphill alongside the forest on a steep slope of grass, bracken and heather. At the top of the slope,

THE IRISH COAST TO COAST WALK

A walker enjoys the view over Lough Tay from the Wicklow Way at Luggala

THE WICKLOW WAY: DAY 3 – KNOCKREE TO LARAGH

cross a stile over a wall on the right and head along a path flanked by heather and bilberry, towards the rounded mountain of **Djouce**. Keep to the clearest path, then consider whether to branch right and make a summit bid, or keep straight on across the upper slopes of the mountain. The Wicklow Way traverses the slope and climbs to a moorland gap at 620m (2035ft), while the summit of Djouce rises to 725m (2385ft). If you climb the mountain, swing left at the summit rocks and trig point to follow a path straight back down towards the Wicklow Way.

Whatever route is chosen, the Wicklow Way crosses boggy ground by following a line of stout railway sleepers. Follow these over **White Hill** at 630m (2075ft), where cotton grass grows, and pass a white outcrop of quartz. The route leads downhill to pass through a gap between two stands of forest, crossing a chunky stile. Another length of railway sleeper path leads round to **Luggala**, where there are increasingly wonderful views of a deep glen and rolling

THE IRISH COAST TO COAST WALK

mountain-moorlands. The Vartry Reservoir and the coast of Co Wicklow are also in view. Take a look at a small memorial stone tucked underneath a granite boulder: 'To the memory of J B Malone – Pioneer of the Wicklow Way'. JB was also known as the 'Walking Encyclopedia'.

WICKLOW MOUNTAINS NATIONAL PARK

The Wicklow Mountains National Park has been created in piecemeal fashion from various properties owned by the State. In effect, the national park is almost entirely State-owned and controlled, and largely covers all the bleak, barren, boggy mountains and moorlands through the heart of the Wicklow Mountains. In its full extent, the national park stretches from Kippure, the highest point in Co Dublin at 757m (2475ft) to Lugnaquillia, the highest point in Co Wicklow at 925m (3039ft). There was once a plan to build a visitor centre near Luggala, but this proved so controversial that the site had to be abandoned even though the initial groundwork had been completed.

Look down into the glen to see **Lough Tay** and a small part of Lough Dan. Walk down wooden steps and turn left at a junction to enter a forest. Turn right and right again to leave the forest, walking through a car park to reach the R759 road. Keep left to walk up the road, then down the road, still with good views into the glen. After passing the **Pier Gates** the road swings left down towards Roundwood, but the Wicklow Way turns right down a forest track at **Sleamaine**, passing a barrier. Keep straight on uphill at a junction, then keep right at another junction. Pass a hut on the way to a heathery gap in the forest. The track climbs across an open slope at **Ballinafunshoge** with views of Roundwood and the Vartry Reservoirs. Go through a gate back into the forest, almost to 440m (1445ft), and later drop downhill. A marker points to the right, indicating a boggy path crossing stones and tree roots. This later drops and there is a view of **Lough Dan** ahead. Turn left along a track, then keep left, then turn right, to follow a track past Forest Way Lodge to a road. If you wish to move off-route to **Roundwood**, do it here, otherwise turn right along the road.

The Wicklow Way: Day 3 – Knockree to Laragh

ROUNDWOOD

Roundwood is a long and straggly village that claims to be the highest in Ireland, standing around 230m (755ft). The huge Vartry Reservoirs near the village supply water to distant Dublin. Roundwood offers a small number of accommodation options, including a campsite. There is a post office, a couple of shops, a few pubs and restaurants, as well as toilets. St Kevin's Bus (tel 01-2828119) operates a daily service through the village, linking with Dublin, Bray, Laragh and Glendalough.

Follow the road downhill through a crossroads at **Baltynanima**, through lovely oakwoods mixed with holly, honeysuckle and bilberry. Cross the Old Bridge over the **Avonmore River** and turn left at a road junction to climb uphill as signposted for Laragh and Glendalough. The steep and winding road passes the Wicklow Way Lodge and there is a shelter belt of fine trees alongside, to the left, including pines, chestnut and beech. Follow the road over a crest and downhill, then uphill again with the shelter belt still running alongside. Turn right at **Pinewood Cottage** and follow a track uphill, passing a house and going through a gate. Continue up the track to reach another gate, the **Brusher Gate**, and turn left. Cross a couple of stiles and walk alongside a forest, then walk through it for a while, then alongside it again. Cross a stile and follow a clear, grassy path across a slope of bracken, grass and heather. Keep right to walk alongside another forest, heading up to 350m (1150ft) on **Paddock Hill**. Walk downhill with views towards the village of Laragh and glorious Glendalough, surrounded by bleak and rugged mountains.

The path drifts away from the forest and crosses a stile on its way downhill. Walk down a slope alongside a young forest, then head down to a track which leads through pleasantly mixed woodlands in **Glenmacnass**. When the R115 road is reached, turn left for a short way, then turn right down a path to reach a footbridge over the bouldery **Glenmacnass River**. The Wicklow Way turns right to continue, but if you wish to visit **Laragh** turn left to reach a track, then left again to head for the village and all its facilities.

LARAGH

The Glendalough Visitor Centre between Laragh and Glandalough

Although recently by-passed by the Wicklow Way, most wayfarers would head into Laragh to avail themselves of its services, and it has a reputation as the gateway to Glendalough. There is plenty of accommodation of all types, but in the height of summer every bed can be taken. There is a post office, a couple of shops, and a few pubs and restaurants. St Kevin's Bus (tel 01–2828119) operates a daily service through the village, linking with Glendalough, Roundwood, Bray and Dublin. Laragh and Glendalough are among the busiest tourist destinations in Ireland, and in the summer months it makes sense to book your accommodation well in advance.

DAY 4
Laragh to Glenmalure

Start	Laragh (grid ref 143966)
Finish	Drumgoff, Glenmalure (grid ref 106909)
Distance	17km (10.5 miles)
Cumulative Distance	76km (47 miles)
Maps	OSI Discovery 56, Harvey Maps' *Wicklow Mountains*
Terrain	Mostly forest tracks, rising to a high, boggy gap before descending.
Refreshments	The Glendalough Hotel has a restaurant. The Lakeside Take Away is at the Upper Lake. The Glenmalure Lodge offers food and drink at the end of the day.

Distractions abound in Glendalough. The ruins of the famous ancient 'seven churches' demand inspection and a visitor centre offers plenty of information about this former monastic city. Delve into the life and times of St Kevin, or look for the burial place of the Kings of Leinster. The scenery is enchanting and the day's walk is short, so there is no need to hurry. In the past, walkers would press on beyond Glenmalure and stay at Aughavannagh Youth Hostel. The hostel is now closed and walkers must either hold back at Glenmalure, walk through an area lacking accommodation, or arrange for a pick-up.

ST KEVIN

St Kevin lived as a hermit in Glendalough in the 6th century; by tradition he slept in a cave, above the Upper Lake, known as St Kevin's Bed. To mortify his flesh he waded into the cold waters of the lake and raised his hands in prayer. So fervently did he pray that he didn't notice a bird building a nest in his outstretched palm. Being a gentle man, he waited until the eggs were hatched and the fledglings flown before leaving the lake. Of such men are legends born and Glendalough duly became a centre of pilgrimage!

The Irish Coast to Coast Walk

The curious church known as St Kevin's Kitchen in the wooded Glendalough

Leave **Laragh** by walking up towards **St Kevin's Church**, then turn right and immediately left to enter a forest. Follow the main forest track until the waymarked Wicklow Way is found again at a point where tracks cross. Walk straight onwards and the track swings right as it climbs. Keep left at another junction; staying on the forest track, not using the track leaving the forest. Climb a little higher, then descend and go through a gateway. A path is worn down to the schist bedrock and it climbs to allow a fine view over dense gorse bushes into **Glendalough**. Walk downhill again into the forest, through a gate and down a track. Watch out on a slope of pines and bracken for a path that heads sharp left and then right to run downhill. Cross a handful of stiles in a short distance to land on the busy R756 road, and cross to the other side with care. A short path leads straight to the **Glendalough Hotel**.

THE WICKLOW WAY: DAY 4 – LARAGH TO GLENMALURE

THE MONASTIC CITY

The small rural monastery at Glendalough was founded in the 7th century and grew until eclipsed by the founding of larger monasteries in the 13th century. In its heyday this monastery was a renowned centre of learning. The *Glendalough Visitor Centre* offers a good grounding in rural Irish monasticism, after which guides are available to lead you through the *Monastic City* nearby. The most popular attractions are the refuge, known as the *Round Tower*, and the curious church known as *St Kevin's Kitchen* (which has a miniature round tower poking from its roof). The *cathedral ruin*, dedicated to St Peter and St Paul, was built in several stages and must have been one of the more ornate structures. It ceased to be a cathedral in 1214. Nearby is the monolithic *St Kevin's Cross*, which may be the oldest monument on the site, sculpted some time between the 6th and 8th centuries. Some say that St Kevin was buried beneath it, while the nearby 12th-century *Priest's House* may have held relics of the saint. The *Gatehouse*, near the Glendalough Hotel, was built in the 10th or 11th century. With a day to spare, leisurely explorations around the floor of the glen could take in a series of ancient church ruins, collectively known as the *'seven churches'*. Before pilgrimages to Glendalough became marred by faction fighting and riots, leading to a complete ban of pilgrims, seven pilgrimages to Glendalough were equal, by curious reckoning, to one pilgrimage to Rome!

The Wicklow Way turns left at the **Glendalough Hotel**, then right for the **Glendalough Visitor Centre**. This is also the main visitor centre for the Wicklow Mountains National Park, and there are toilets on site. Walk across the floor of the glen and cross a wooden bridge over the river. Turn right along a broad track signposted as the

GLENDALOUGH

If you prefer to be away from the bustling village of Laragh, there are a few good facilities around Glendalough. Accommodation options include the Glendalough Hotel, a few B&Bs and a youth hostel. The only shop mostly sells souvenirs, but also offers tourist information, and there is a take-away near the Upper Lake. St Kevin's Bus (tel 01–2828119) links Glendalough daily with Laragh, Roundwood, Bray and Dublin.

THE IRISH COAST TO COAST WALK

Walkers take a break just off-route to admire the Upper Lake in Glendalough

THE WICKLOW WAY: DAY 4 – LARAGH TO GLENMALURE

Green Road to the Upper Lake. There is another bridge giving access to the Monastic City if you wish to make another visit. Have a look at a notice explaining about the Glendalough Woods Nature Reserve, pass the Lower Lake and continue along the track to pass the **Information Office**. This little building is full of nature notes and is worth investigating when open. The Upper Lake is nearby, but slightly off-route, though a detour is worth it for the view.

Turn left as marked, and walk across a wooden bridge, then up a track and a flight of steps signposted for **Poulanass Waterfall**. Admire the falls on the way uphill, then turn left along a track, and left again to cross two bridges over two

THE IRISH COAST TO COAST WALK

Poulanass Waterfall is passed as the Wicklow Way climbs from Glendalough

The Wicklow Way used to cross the 657m (2179ft) summit in its early days, and a detour can be made if you wish to include a visit.

streams that flow close together. A small wall beside the second bridge has a handful of geological specimens built into it. Follow the track uphill, then turn right at a junction and keep climbing. The track later swings right and undulates after crossing **Lugduff Brook**. Pass a vague junction, then turn left at a clearer junction. Continue uphill until the track bends left, then turn right at yet another junction. Keep climbing almost to a gap outside the forest, where you turn left towards the rounded summit of **Mullacor**. ◀

Turn right along a path made of stout railway sleepers, and keep left at a junction to follow the path across the gap of **Borenacrow** at 550m (1800ft). The

THE WICKLOW WAY: DAY 4 – LARAGH TO GLENMALURE

huge, sprawling mountain-moorland of Lugnaquillia, the highest in Co Wicklow at 925m (3039ft), blocks views on the other side of Glenmalure. Wooden steps leads down to a forest, where the path swings left alongside. Traverse a slope of grass and bilberry, which may be boggy in places, then drop steeply down towards the forest and walk down through it. The path can be muddy, with exposed tree roots and rocks, so take care.

Turn left down a forest track, then right at the next junction, then keep left as marked and enjoy fine views over **Glenmalure**. Zig-zag right and left onto a lower

The route passes through working forests as it crosses Glenmalure

THE MILITARY ROAD

For many centuries the Wicklow Mountains were well beyond the 'pale'. English influence from Dublin held little sway over the area as the O'Byrnes held the glens for their own, and were well able to repel any forces that were sent into the mountains. In 1580 an English force was dispatched to Glenmalure and were roundly defeated, with Edmund Spenser and Walter Raleigh being among those fleeing for their lives!

It was the 1798 Rebellion that finally brought changes into the Wicklow Mountains. As English forces were once more at a distinct disadvantage in this bleak and remote terrain, steps were taken to tame the wilderness once and for all, with soldiers and navvies labouring over the mountains in the early 1800s laying the military road over the bogs and round the mountainsides. They penetrated the remotest glens and a series of barracks were constructed at strategic points such as Glencree, Laragh, Glenmalure and Aughavannagh. Each of the barracks' buildings have had chequered careers. The one at Glencree served as a reformatory and a centre for Christian reconciliation. The one at Laragh was completely demolished. Glenmalure's old barracks lie derelict. The same fate may befall the one at Aughavannagh, which served as a shooting lodge and youth hostel, though it is now closed and in a dangerous state. The military road is signposted as a 'scenic drive' and offers access to a number of splendid walking throughout the Wicklow Mountains.

track and follow this onwards. It later swings left away from Glenmalure above **Cullen's Rock**. Walk down to another junction and turn right, heading back into Glenmalure. Walk down to the **military road** where **Coolalingo Bridge** crosses a river. Turn right downhill, then at a crossroads the Wicklow Way runs straight through. However, walkers taking a break at this point will find the Glenmalure Lodge and Coolalingo B&B are just off to the left. Think twice about continuing further, as there is no accommodation, food or drink to be found near the route for some time.

DAY 5
Glenmalure to Tinahely

Start	Drumgoff, Glenmalure (grid ref 106909)
Finish	Tinahely (grid ref 036731)
Distance	36km (22.5 miles)
Cumulative Distance	112km (69.5 miles)
Maps	OSI Discovery 56 & 62
Terrain	Mostly forest tracks though hilly country, then minor roads through Moyne. Grassy hill tracks and paths are used at the end of the day.
Refreshments	None after leaving Glenmalure. Pubs at Knockananna are off-route. There are a few pubs at the end of the day in Tinahely.

This is a long day's walk, passing through a quiet area where accommodation is sparse. If you think it may be too far to Tinahely note that there are a couple of B&Bs off-route before that point, not far from the tiny village of Moyne. Alternatively, phone around to find someone who will collect you from some point along the way, then drop you back on the route the next day. The Wicklow Way is mostly routed along forest tracks where a brisk pace can be adopted, then a quiet road leads to Moyne. A scenic walk along grassy tracks around a gentle hillside overlooks Tinahely towards the end of the day.

Follow the military road away from **Glenmalure** as signposted for Rathdangan and Aughrim. Cross the **Avonbeg River** and note the derelict barracks building on the left. Turn right along a track as signposted for the Wicklow Way and cross a stream. Fork left through a gate, then walk up into a forest. Swing left and climb, then swing right. Climb further and swing right, then climb again and turn left. Walk downhill to cross the **Clohernagh Brook**, then follow a pleasant grassy track. Watch carefully for a

THE IRISH COAST TO COAST WALK

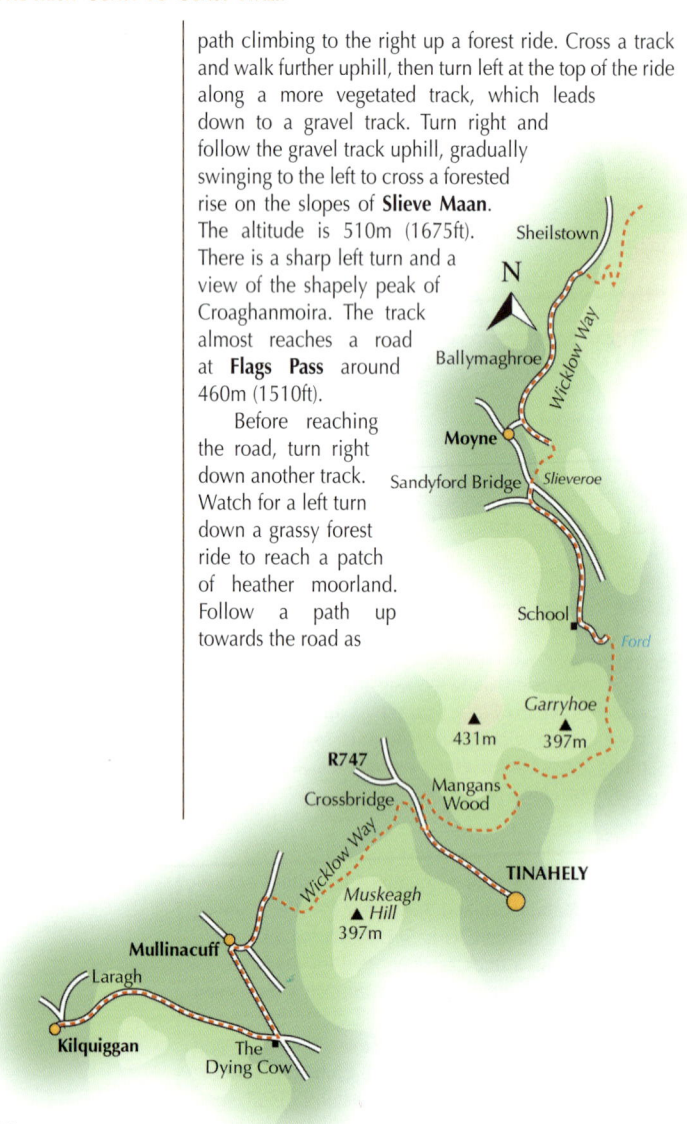

path climbing to the right up a forest ride. Cross a track and walk further uphill, then turn left at the top of the ride along a more vegetated track, which leads down to a gravel track. Turn right and follow the gravel track uphill, gradually swinging to the left to cross a forested rise on the slopes of **Slieve Maan**. The altitude is 510m (1675ft). There is a sharp left turn and a view of the shapely peak of Croaghanmoira. The track almost reaches a road at **Flags Pass** around 460m (1510ft).

Before reaching the road, turn right down another track. Watch for a left turn down a grassy forest ride to reach a patch of heather moorland. Follow a path up towards the road as

THE WICKLOW WAY: DAY 5 – GLENMALURE TO TINAHELY

marked, then turn right to walk parallel to the road and largely out of sight of it. Come onto the road to cross a small stream in a steep-sided little valley, then walk down the road a bit. The Wicklow Way is signposted up to the left along a forest track. Keep straight on at a junction, then stay on the clearest track climbing uphill to almost 500m (1640ft) on **Carrickashane Mountain**. Walk steeply downhill, then keep left and walk further downhill and along a track. There is a slight ascent, then the track swings round the forested slope before descending again. Turn right downhill at a junction to reach a barrier at a road. Turn right down the road as signposted, parallel to **Mucklagh Brook** deep in the valley. Head off to the left as signposted down another forest track. Turn right at the bottom to reach the **Iron Bridge** over the Ow River.

Cross the Iron Bridge and enjoy views back to the higher Wicklow Mountains from a strip of green pasture between the forests that flank the valley. The road leads up to a farmhouse where you turn left at a junction. Later, branch right up a track, rising across a forested slope to reach a higher road. Turn left to cross **Ballyteige Bridge**, then turn right past a barrier to walk up a forest track. Keep to the track overlooking the valley and stream until you can swing left at the top to traverse the forested

The pleasant, pastoral Ow Valley with a view back to broad Lugnaquillia

61

THE IRISH COAST TO COAST WALK

slopes of **Sheilstown Hill**. The track rises to 400m (1310ft), then falls gently. A zig-zag leads right, left and right again down to a barrier and another quiet road. There are views back to the sprawling slopes of Lugnaquillia; now looking rather distant.

Turn left along the road. There are two roads dropping off to the right later; the latter one leads into the tiny village of **Moyne**. Use this if heading off-route to Jigsaw Cottage B&B, or well off-route to the village of Knockananna to reach a shop and pubs, otherwise walk straight onwards. The road climbs from Moyne, but a grassy lane heads down to the right, becoming stony towards the bottom. Turn left along a road, then right as signposted for the Wicklow Way. This road is also signposted for Rathshanmore and Kyle Farmhouse B&B. Pass a farm and cross **Sandyford Bridge**, then turn left along another quiet road (signposted for the Wicklow Way and Tinahely) running through a pleasant valley.

Follow the undulating road gradually uphill, keeping left and passing an old **school**, before dropping steeply towards a **bridge** and a river. Don't cross the bridge, but turn right to ford a lesser stream; though one that will result in wet feet in wet weather. A lane flanked by tangled hedgerows can be muddy as it climbs uphill, but

Crossing a small stream on the slopes of Garryhoe on the way to Tinahely

THE WICKLOW WAY: DAY 5 – GLENMALURE TO TINAHELY

once it passes through a gate it becomes delightfully grassy as it continues across the bracken slopes of **Garryhoe**. There are fine views back to Sheilstown Hill and Croaghanmoira, with Croaghaun also prominently in view. Simply follow the grassy track as it winds and rolls, generally rising, then the view back includes distant Lugnaquillia. Watch for a branch to the right leading uphill, to around 290m (950ft). ▶ Walk along the track and note the **Doctor's Cross**, built in memory of a local doctor who died after a shooting accident on this spot. There is a fine view ahead to the Blackstairs Mountains, which will be reached over the next few days.

The left branch leads off-route to accommodation at Rosbane Farmhouse B&B.

As the track begins to descend, watch for a glimpse of Tinahely nestling in a fold in the hills. Turn right at a junction and walk along a track to a gate and stile. Follow the track down through a plantation of beeches at **Mangans Wood**. Cross a stile beside a gate at the bottom and turn right along another track. Go through a gate to walk along a grassy track called **Coolafunshoge Lane**, passing through a handful of other gates in turn, avoiding the fields to right and left. There is another glimpse of Tinahely down to the left, but keep following the track round the hillside. When a road is reached, turn left downhill, crossing a bridge by a ford over the **Derry River**. Turn left to walk road with care along the R747. The Wicklow Way turns right uphill at a junction with a narrow road, but most wayfarers will continue straight onwards into **Tinahely** to avail themselves of its welcome range of services.

TINAHELY

Tinahely was wrecked during the 1798 Rebellion, but is now a fine little Georgian town with three roads branching from a large, central triangular area. The most prominent building is the Tinahely Courthouse Centre. Accommodation is limited to a few B&Bs. There is a bank with ATM, post office, a few shops, pubs and restaurants. Bus Éireann table number 132 serves Tinahely from Dublin on Thursday, Friday and Sunday. There is also a Rural Bus service on Saturday.

The Irish Coast to Coast Walk

DAY 6
Tinahely to Clonegal

Start	Tinahely (grid ref 036731)
Finish	Clonegal (grid ref 914613)
Distance	34km (21 miles)
Cumulative Distance	146km (90.5 miles)
Maps	OSI Discovery 61 & 62
Terrain	Mostly along minor roads, but some forest tracks and field paths.
Refreshments	The Dying Cow pub at Stranakelly Crossroads, pubs and shops off-route at Shillelagh and Parkbridge and shops and pubs at Clonegal.

If attempts are made to shorten this long day's walk, as well as the previous long day's walk, you might need to arrange a pick-up and drop-off with a nearby accommodation provider. Most of the day is spent trudging up and down quiet minor roads, though there are some stretches along field paths and forest tracks. Be warned that some of the field paths can be very muddy when wet. The Wicklow Way is quite convoluted over Stookeen Hill and Urelands Hill, so keep an eye on the marker posts and the route description. If you only intend following the course of the Wicklow Way for the time being, then most accommodation providers will be happy to give you a lift to Bunclody if you wish to catch a bus out of the area and back to Dublin.

Follow the busy R747, or Hacketstown road, back out of **Tinahely** to pick up the course of the Wicklow Way again. Branch left up a minor road and pass **Ashfield B&B**. Turn left as signposted for the Wicklow Way; not up a track, but up a narrow path flanked by hedgerows. Turn left at a gate, walk up a track to another gate, then turn slightly right to follow a grassy, sunken way flanked by gorse bushes. Follow this route generally uphill through a few

THE WICKLOW WAY: DAY 6 – TINAHELY TO CLONEGAL

gates on the slopes of **Muskeagh Hill**. Avoid any gates leading into fields below the track, and rise gradually to 240m (785ft). Eventually, swing right down to a track, then turn left to walk alongside a plantation of beeches. Another right turn leads down through fields to a road. There are fine views back towards Lugnaquillia and the Wicklow Mountains.

Turn left to follow the road, then at the bottom, turn right and walk straight through a junction at **Mullinacuff**. Turn left before the little Church of Ireland building, then follow the road onwards and gradually uphill to reach Stranakelly Crossroads. There is a tiny pub on a farm here, known as **The Dying Cow**. ▶

Turn right up another road to leave the pub, crossing the hillside around 230m (755ft), then dropping downhill to cross a stream in a valley. Turn left at a crossroads to reach St Finian's Church in the scattered village of **Kilquiggan**. Pass a school and continue along the road. Turn right and immediately left at a staggered crossroads as signposted for the Wicklow Way and Clonegal. Walk up the road and turn left, then from a crest on the road at **Boley** there is a view back to Lugnaquillia, rising far

An old grassy track flanked by gorse bushes is followed across Muskeagh Hill

Apparently, the police visited late one night, and the landlady at the time objected, saying that she wasn't serving drink after hours, but only providing refreshments to neighbours who were helping her with a dying cow!

THE IRISH COAST TO COAST WALK

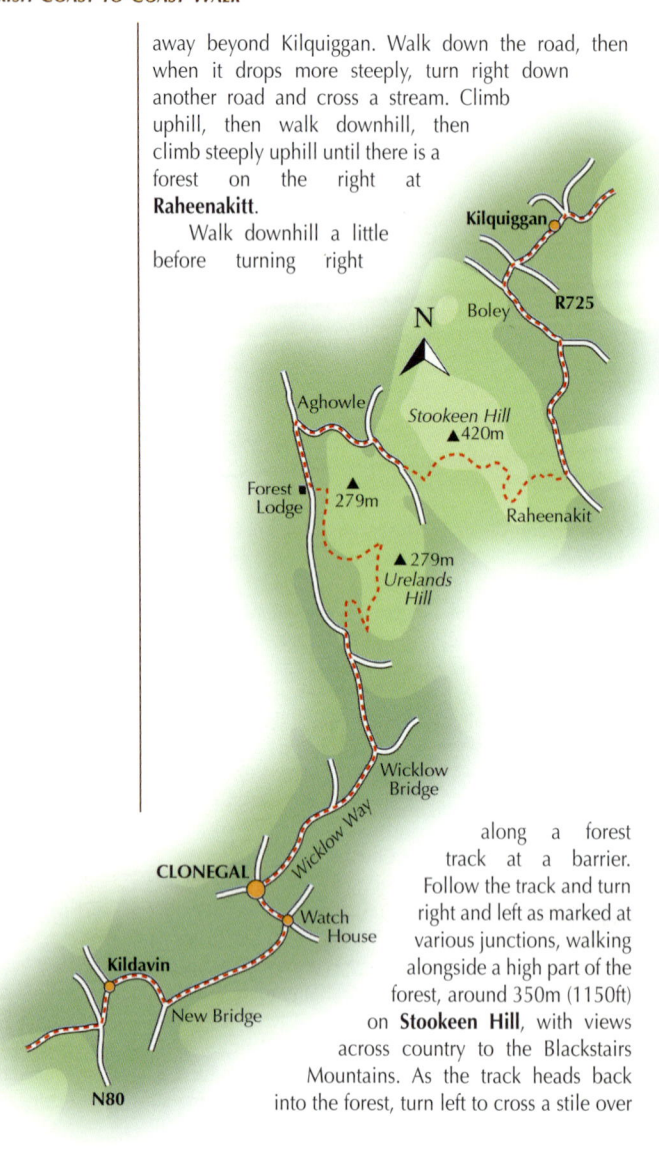

away beyond Kilquiggan. Walk down the road, then when it drops more steeply, turn right down another road and cross a stream. Climb uphill, then walk downhill, then climb steeply uphill until there is a forest on the right at **Raheenakitt**.

Walk downhill a little before turning right along a forest track at a barrier. Follow the track and turn right and left as marked at various junctions, walking alongside a high part of the forest, around 350m (1150ft) on **Stookeen Hill**, with views across country to the Blackstairs Mountains. As the track heads back into the forest, turn left to cross a stile over

The Wicklow Way: Day 6 – Tinahely to Clonegal

a fence and walk down a path alongside the forest. The path broadens and lands on a good, clear track. Turn right to follow the track down to a road, then turn right along the road at **Aghowle**. Turn left at a junction and follow a winding road to another junction to turn left again. Follow the road to **Forest Lodge**.

A Wicklow Way signpost points left through a gate into a forest on the slopes of **Moylisha Hill**. Follow a forest track gently uphill, noting how much beech grows among the conifers. Turn right at a junction, then later make a right and left in quick succession to climb higher. Take another left turn and enjoy views back across to Stookeen Hill before turning right. There are views of the Blackstairs Mountains from the track, which runs at about 260m (850ft) across the slopes of **Urelands Hill**. Trees close off the views as the track drops gradually down to a junction. Turn right and follow the track down through mixed woodlands to reach a barrier. Turn left down the access road leading away from **Urelands House** to reach a road.

The church at Kilquiggan is located a short distance outside the village

67

THE IRISH COAST TO COAST WALK

Haymaking in the fields around Clonegal at the end of the Wicklow Way

Turn left, then right in quick succession down roads. Keep right again at a later junction to cross **Wicklow Bridge**. Although the bridge is hardly noticed, it marks the point where you pass from Co Wicklow to Co Carlow. Continue along the road through a verdant valley, with the Blackstairs Mountains often in view. The road leads into the little village of **Clonegal**, which is at the end of the Wicklow Way, where most walkers would be ready to take a break.

CLONEGAL

Clonegal is a particularly tidy village, with a small green and a Wicklow Way mapboard. There is also a pleasant space to sit down beside the Derry River. The older buildings in the village have interesting architectural features, while Huntington Castle stands retired from the road. The *Clonegal 1798 Hanging Stone* recalls the strife associated with the 1798 Rebellion, which was particularly fierce in the south-east of Ireland.

Facilities in Clonegal include only a couple of B&Bs, so be prepared to phone around other addresses in the countryside. There is a post office, a couple of shops and pubs, but no bus services. Local accommodation providers are usually happy to run walkers to Bunclody to catch a bus.

STAGE 2
The South Leinster Way

High on the slopes of Mount Alto, looking back towards rounded Brandon Hill (Day 9)

THE IRISH COAST TO COAST WALK

DAY 7
Clonegal to Borris

Start	Clonegal (grid ref 914613)
Finish	Borris (grid ref 730504)
Distance	26km (16 miles)
Cumulative Distance	172km (106.5 miles)
Maps	OSI Discovery 61 & 68
Terrain	Forest tracks are used on the initial ascent, then the rest of the day's walk is along roads across moorland slopes or through farmland
Refreshments	There are no shops or pubs between Kildavin and Borris

There is a short road-walk without waymarks between the end of the Wicklow Way at Clonegal and the start of the South Leinster Way at Kildavin. A farm road and forest tracks then lead up to a scenic road that crosses the high moorland slopes of Mount Leinster. Another road leads to a transmitter mast on top of the mountain, making this the highest point in Ireland that can be gained with relative ease. Despite the intrusive nature of the mast, the summit makes a fine viewpoint in clear weather and may well be worth the detour. Roads lead all the way down to Borris; a fine old estate village near Borris House.

Follow the road signposted for Bunclody to leave **Clonegal**, crossing a five-arched stone bridge over the **Derry River**. Crossing the river takes you from Co Carlow into Co Wexford, and the small settlement up at a crossroads is the **Watch House**. The *Watch House Forge Stone* at the crossroads is another reminder of the 1798 Rebellion. Turn right to leave the village and note the occasional glimpses of the Derry River from the road. Later, turn right to cross back from Co Wexford to Co Carlow, using the **New Bridge** spanning the **River Slaney**, just below its confluence with the Derry River. Follow the

SOUTH LEINSTER WAY: DAY 7 – CLONEGAL TO BORRIS

road round Ally Hore's Corner and up past the GAA grounds to reach the little village of **Kildavin**.

KILDAVIN

Kildavin is the true start of the South Leinster Way, and the first signposts for the route stand in front of the Church of Ireland, along with a mapboard. Facilities in the village are limited to Conway's Bar Lounge and a post office shop. Bus Éireann services used to stop in the village, but now hurtle along the busy N80 by-pass to nearby Bunclody, where table number 5 offers daily links with Dublin and Waterford. There is no accommodation in the village, but local providers are usually happy to pick-up and drop-off walkers in Kildavin, or at nearby Bunclody if they are using the bus.

Conway's Bar Lounge at the start of the South Leinster Way, in Kildavin

THE IRISH COAST TO COAST WALK

Turn left by Conway's Bar to leave **Kildavin**, following what was once the main road towards Bunclody. Cross the busy N80 by-pass with care and walk up the narrow **Ballypierce Lane**. Some of the houses along the lane have their names inscribed on big boulders of granite. Towards the end of the road the **Mount Leinster Cottages** are passed. Turn left here, up a track covered in large stones, and follow it as it bends to the left towards a forest. Turn sharp right at a junction, and the track later levels out and leaves the forest briefly while it crosses a steep slope of bracken and heather on **Greenoge Hill**.

Back in the forest, the track leads gradually up to a gap where the trees are briefly pinched out and there are views of the moorland slopes either side of **Kilbrannish Hill**. Take a last look back to Kildavin and the Wicklow Mountains, and cross straight over the gap to walk downhill. The huge bulk of Mount Leinster is seen ahead. Keep to the clearest track, avoiding other tracks, all the way down to a barrier and a road. Turn right along the road towards **Corrabut Gap** on the Mount Leinster Drive, but turn left along a road signposted for the Nine Stones before reaching the gap. The road leaves the forest

SOUTH LEINSTER WAY: DAY 7 – CLONEGAL TO BORRIS

and climbs steadily round a huge hollow on the slopes of Mount Leinster. A gap is reached around 440m (1450ft) at the **Nine Stones**. There are views beyond the gap and the Nine Stones to Brandon Hill and Slievenamon, with the Comeragh and Knockmealdown Mountains seen between, towards which the Coast to Coast Walk is heading.

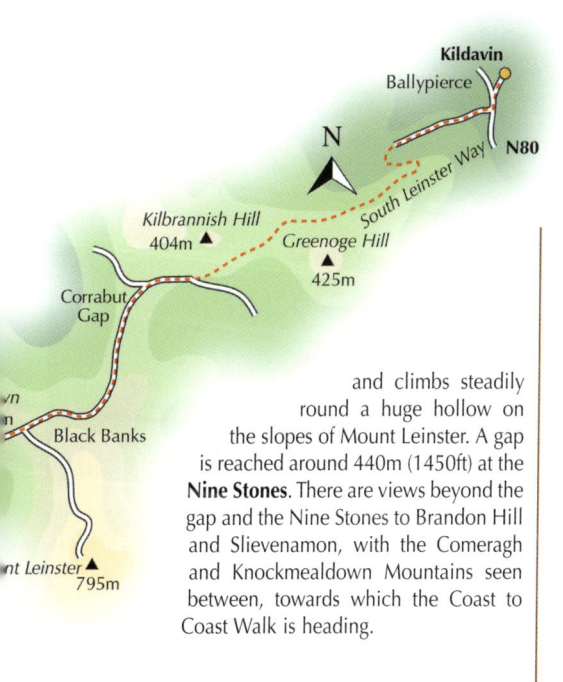

MOUNT LEINSTER

The Nine Stones are supposedly an ancient alignment of stones beside the road on the high gap, but they don't look particularly convincing. Across the road, a sign beside a gate announces that the Mount Leinster Transmitting Station is the property of Radio Telefís Éireann, that the summit of the mountain rises to 795m (2610ft), and that the mast itself is a further 122m (400ft) high. Walkers can use the road to the mast to get to and from the summit with comparative ease, though it is a journey of 5km (3 miles) there and back. In clear weather a detour is recommended for the extensive view, which can stretch far beyond the south-east of Ireland to the distant hills of Co Clare. The lower hill of Slievebawn, rising to 525m (1727ft) can also be climbed with ease from the Nine Stones in a journey of 2km (1.25 miles) there-and-back.

The bleak Blackstairs Mountains seen near the Nine Stones on Mount Leinster

Walk down the road with forest to the left and the heathery slopes of **Slievebawn** to the right. The slopes are occasionally studded with prominent boulders of white quartz. There are farms and houses along the way, then you reach a crossroads, where there is an old water pump, at **Tomduff**.

Walk straight through as signposted for Borris, and walk straight across a nearby crossroads too. Continue along the road as marked, making a right turn at a junction. Shortly afterwards, turn down to the left, bearing in mind the marker may be hidden. Again, shortly afterwards, turn right and walk straight onwards at the next junction. **Spahill Cross Roads** has signposts and a right turn leads across **Bowe's Bridge**. Take a look back towards the rugged flanks of the Blackstairs Mountains. The road passes beneath an arch on an old railway viaduct (which can be mounted and walked end-to-end). At a junction with the R702 road, simply turn right and walk up the road through **Borris** to avail yourself of all its facilities. Halfway through the village, there is a narrow strip of land between the demesne wall of Borris House and the road, which makes a fine little linear park.

BORRIS

The post office in the estate village of Borris has a fine traditional shop front

Borris is forever associated with the MacMurrough Kavanaghs; a family descended from the Kings of Leinster. Their ancestral seat is Borris House, hidden in a wooded demesne behind a stout wall. The family featured several remarkable characters through the centuries. Art was poisoned in 1417 and his funeral cortege stretched for 10km (6 miles) along the road from New Ross to St Mullins. Morgan was a giant of a man who served the King of Prussia for a time. The king was reluctant to let him go home, but Morgan said he would bring his brothers back, who he claimed were even bigger men. The king reluctantly let him go, and never saw him again! Arthur was born in 1831 without arms or legs, yet he became an accomplished rider, hunter and Member of Parliament, as well as a traveller of the world.

Facilities at Borris include only a couple of B&Bs, a bank with an ATM, post office, a few shops, pubs and restaurants. Call Ring a Link (tel 1890–424141) for details of local bus connections.

THE IRISH COAST TO COAST WALK

DAY 8
Borris to Inistioge

Start	Borris (grid ref 730504)
Finish	Inistioge (grid ref 635377)
Distance	28km (17.5 miles)
Cumulative Distance	200km (124 miles)
Map	OSI Discovery 68
Terrain	After an initial road-walk, a grassy riverside towpath is followed. Another stretch along roads is proceeded by forest tracks and farm tracks.
Refreshments	There are plenty of shops, bars and restaurants in Graiguenamanagh

After leaving Borris the South Leinster Way runs in common with the Barrow Way, heading along the lovely grassy towpath of the River Barrow. Enjoy the sights of barges and cruisers navigating the river and negotiating the locks between Borris and Graiguenamanagh. The bustling little town of Graiguenamanagh partly faces the River Barrow but also huddles close to the ancient abbey, from which it derives its name. Rising above the town is Brandon Hill, and the South Leinster Way uses a variety of forest tracks to traverse its slopes. At the end of the day, the charming village of Inistioge is found beside the River Nore, centred on a fine green.

Walk up the R702 road through **Borris**, alongside the demesne wall and out of the village. Turn left at a junction as signposted for Graiguenamanagh and follow the bendy road down to the River Barrow at **Ballyteigelea Bridge**. Don't cross the bridge, but walk down to the left to reach the river and towpath. Turn left to follow the broad, level and grassy towpath downstream. On a fine day this is a delightful stretch of the route, with the river to the right and a wetland area to the left. Pass a wooded

SOUTH LEINSTER WAY: DAY 8 – BORRIS TO INISTIOGE

A classic view of a short side-canal on the River Barrow at Clashganna Lock

THE IRISH COAST TO COAST WALK

> There is also a classic view of the River Barrow available from the R729 road high above the river, though the viewpoint can only be reached by making a detour from the route.

island, then pass a weir, noting how a side-channel leads to **Borris Lock** and its old lock-keeper's cottage. Continue downstream around gentle bends with woodlands alongside. Cross the inflowing **Mountain River** using Bunnahown Bridge. Pass another weir and lock-keeper's cottage at **Ballynagrane Lock**. A more open stretch of the river, with glimpses of nearby hills, leads to yet another weir and lock-keeper's cottage at **Clashganna Lock**. Looking back, there is a view of Mount Leinster. ◄

RIVER BARROW

The 'Lordly Barrow' is the second longest river in Ireland after the mighty Shannon. It rises in the middle of the country in the Slieve Bloom and flows southwards to reach the sea at Waterford Harbour. It is very popular with pleasure cruisers; both the gleaming modern vessels and the traditional blue and white Celtic Canal Cruisers from Tullamore. The towpath of the River Barrow has been designated as the Barrow Way, and in fact, an Act of Parliament of 1537 required that 'seven feet of plaine ground' be reserved alongside the river as a towpath and for general access. The Barrow Way links with the Grand Canal Way at Lowtown, which in turn links with Dublin, so that there is a natural low-level alternative route from Dublin to Graiguenamanagh in addition to the waymarked route in this guidebook.

Another side-channel leads to the double **Ballykeenan Lock** and the old lock-keeper's cottage. Follow the river as it bends through a wooded valley, with a glimpse of Brandon Hill ahead, before Graiguenamanagh comes into view. A seven-arched stone bridge leads into the busy little town, and you pass from Co Carlow to Co Kilkenny. ◄ Most walkers would be happy to walk straight into **Graiguenamanagh**, but the waymarked route turns left at the Market Square, then right, then left up the High Street to leave town without making the most of its abundant facilities.

> Crown forces blew up the first arch on the bridge in the 1798 Rebellion, to safeguard the road to Kilkenny.

Follow High Street, or the New Ross road, to leave **Graiguenamanagh**. When the road levels out at the top of town, turn right as signposted for Inistioge. Walk up the

SOUTH LEINSTER WAY: DAY 8 – BORRIS TO INISTIOGE

GRAINUENAMANAGH

The main site of interest is Duiske Abbey, founded by the Cistercians in 1204. After the Dissolution of the 16th century, the abbey decayed and much of the stonework was pillaged for other buildings around town. In 1813 the original abbey church was re-roofed and other restoration work was completed around the building. The full extent of the original abbey is now long buried beneath the narrow streets around town. Many of Graiguenamanagh's businesses have traditional frontages and stand cheek by jowl in a delightfully haphazard fashion. Facilities include a small range of accommodation, a bank with ATM, post office, several shops, pubs and restaurants. Most of the shops and pubs are arranged along Main Street, while Duiske Glass is found on High Street. Call Ring a Link (tel 1890–424141) for details of local bus connections.

Looking across the River Barrow before crossing over to Graiguenamanagh

THE IRISH COAST TO COAST WALK

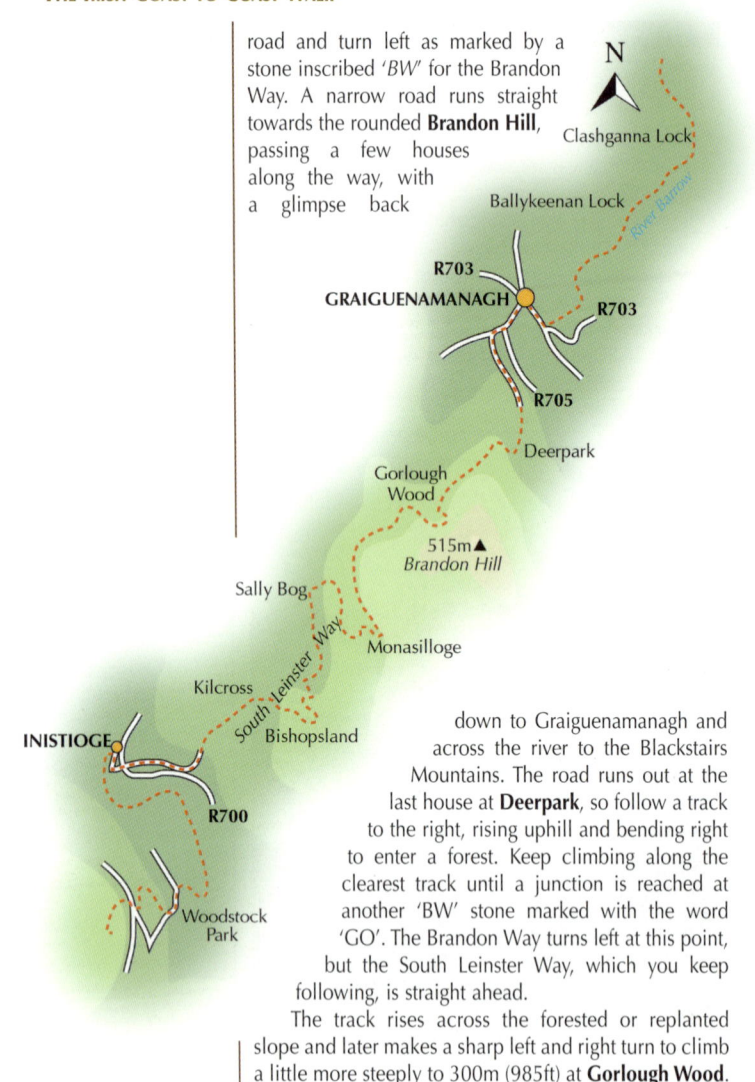

road and turn left as marked by a stone inscribed *'BW'* for the Brandon Way. A narrow road runs straight towards the rounded **Brandon Hill**, passing a few houses along the way, with a glimpse back down to Graiguenamanagh and across the river to the Blackstairs Mountains. The road runs out at the last house at **Deerpark**, so follow a track to the right, rising uphill and bending right to enter a forest. Keep climbing along the clearest track until a junction is reached at another 'BW' stone marked with the word 'GO'. The Brandon Way turns left at this point, but the South Leinster Way, which you keep following, is straight ahead.

The track rises across the forested or replanted slope and later makes a sharp left and right turn to climb a little more steeply to 300m (985ft) at **Gorlough Wood**. (There is a left turn marked for the 'Brandon Hill Cross'

South Leinster Way: Day 8 – Borris to Inistioge

BRANDON HILL

This rounded hill rises to 515m (1703ft) above Graiguenamanagh and the River Barrow, bearing a cross of recent origin. It is the highest hill in Co Kilkenny. Brandon Hill can be climbed from the South Leinster Way by following a signposted route, while the circular Brandon Way is waymarked all around its slopes by chunky stone plinths inscribed with 'BW'. Brandon Hill was once a renowned game reserve and was popular with hunters and poachers. An event remembered as the 'Brandon Shootings' recalls a scuffle between four gamekeepers and three poachers which resulted in a death on either side. Walkers these days will encounter no such problems wandering over the heathery heights, though it can be a featureless place in poor visibility, and the rugged slopes falling down towards the River Barrow should be avoided.

if anyone wishes to make a summit bid.) Follow the track downhill to a junction, then turn left up to a gate and stile. The track runs across the open moorland slopes at the back of Brandon Hill, then another gate

Fields and rugged moorland slopes on the Inistioge side of Brandon Hill

leads back into the forest. Climb again up a clear-felled and replanted slope, then cross another open slope around 300m (985ft) with views ahead to the Comeragh Mountains and Slievenamon.

Walk back into the forest along an undulating track, which suddenly makes a sharp right turn downhill from **Monasilloge**. Turn left at the next junction, then right, then follow a long stretch of track downhill. The track later bends left to reach a point where tracks cross at an intersection near **Sally Bog**. Go straight through, still heading gently downhill. Keep left along the clearest track at the next two junctions, then let the track lead you uphill in lazy loops on a clear-felled and replanted slope to reach 220m (720ft) at **Bishopsland**. Leave the forest through a gate and keep right twice along a track beside the forest fence.

Turn left to follow a narrow, overgrown and possibly muddy track away from the forest. This joins a firmer track that is followed down to the left. Keep heading downhill, avoiding gates leading into fields, and eventually pass a house and reach a road at **Kilcross**. Turn left and walk down the road, then turn right at the bottom. Follow the road uphill until another junction is reached close to Norebridge House B&B. Go straight down a bit of old road blocked by bollards, cross the fine arched bridge over the **River Nore** and walk into the middle of **Inistioge**.

INISTIOGE

Inistioge originally grew around a small monastic site that was associated with a salmon fishery on the River Nore. The pleasant little village stands four-square around a well-tended central green planted with trees and monuments. There is another fine green beside the river. Some of the frontages of the buildings were altered during the filming of 'Circle of Friends', based on the book by Maeve Binchy. Facilities are few but adequate, with a post office, a couple of shops, pubs and restaurants and a handful of B&Bs available. Bus Éireann table number 374 is a Thursday-only service linking Inistioge with New Ross and Kilkenny.

DAY 9
Inistioge to Mullinavat

Start	Inistioge (grid ref 635377)
Finish	Mullinavat (grid ref 564247)
Distance	30km (18.75 miles)
Cumulative Distance	230km (142.75 miles)
Maps	OSI Discovery 68 & 76
Terrain	Mostly forest tracks and minor roads
Refreshments	There is a pub at Lukeswell on the way to Mullinavat

After wandering downstream alongside the River Nore, the South Leinster Way follows a very convoluted course along forest tracks over Mount Alto. After passing through Glenpipe, a more direct route is taken over a broad forested rise. There are virtually no facilities along the way during this day's walk, though there is a pub and B&B at Lukeswell before a road is followed to Mullinavat. The long and straggly village of Mullinavat has rather limited accommodation, so it may be a good idea to book a bed in advance, though regular bus services can be used to reach places with a greater range of facilities.

Leave the green in the middle of Inistioge as signposted for the South Leinster Way and the Riverside Walk. The River Gate leads onto the Point Road, which itself leads to the restored Point Quay on the **River Nore**. The river is actually tidal at this point, though you are a long way from the open sea, and even further away from the end of the Coast to Coast Walk (which isn't even half completed at this stage!). There is a view back towards Inistioge, as well as a nearby memorial recording the tragic drowning of four teenagers. Follow a track roughly parallel to the river and pass a stout old Ice House, which once served nearby **Woodstock House**.

THE IRISH COAST TO COAST WALK

RIVER NORE

The River Nore, along with the Barrow and Suir, flows towards the sea at Waterford Harbour. Collectively they are known as the 'Three Sisters of Ireland'. According to an ancient legend, all the great rivers in Ireland had their source at a single, sacred well; Connle's Well in the Slieve Bloom. It began to flow on the night that Conn of the Hundred Battles was born. Magical hazels overhung the well and crimson nuts which fell into the water were eaten by the Salmon of Knowledge. This should all indicate the reverence shown towards wells and water many centuries ago. Occasional cruisers navigate the tidal reaches of the River Nore, but although a mooring is available near Inistioge, only long-experienced navigators tend to reach it.

Walk along the track and avoid any paths going down to the riverside. The route has been blasted from the rock in places, and the surrounding trees often shield the river from view. Walk past a **house** and keep straight on at a junction of tracks. At length another junction is reached and the track ahead is marked as a cul-de-sac. Turn right and follow a track in a sweeping bend uphill through the forest around **Woodstock Park**. Turn left as marked, then right to reach an 'island' of trees at a junction with a road.

Turn left up the road for a while, then right along a clear track. This descends gently, then bends left uphill. Turn right up another road and quickly reach a junction, then turn left up a broad forest track. Turn left at the next two junctions with tracks, then right at the one following. The track bends to the right and crosses the crest of

WOODSTOCK HOUSE

Woodstock House, a property of the Tighe family, was burnt during the Troubles of the 1920s. Paths were laid out around the demesne in the 18th century and some of these can still be followed through woodlands. More extensive forests were planted in the 20th century. The formal gardens belonging to the house are splendid and can be visited by making a detour. The Ice House that belonged to Woodstock House now houses a colony of bats.

SOUTH LEINSTER WAY: DAY 9 – INISTIOGE TO MULLINAVAT

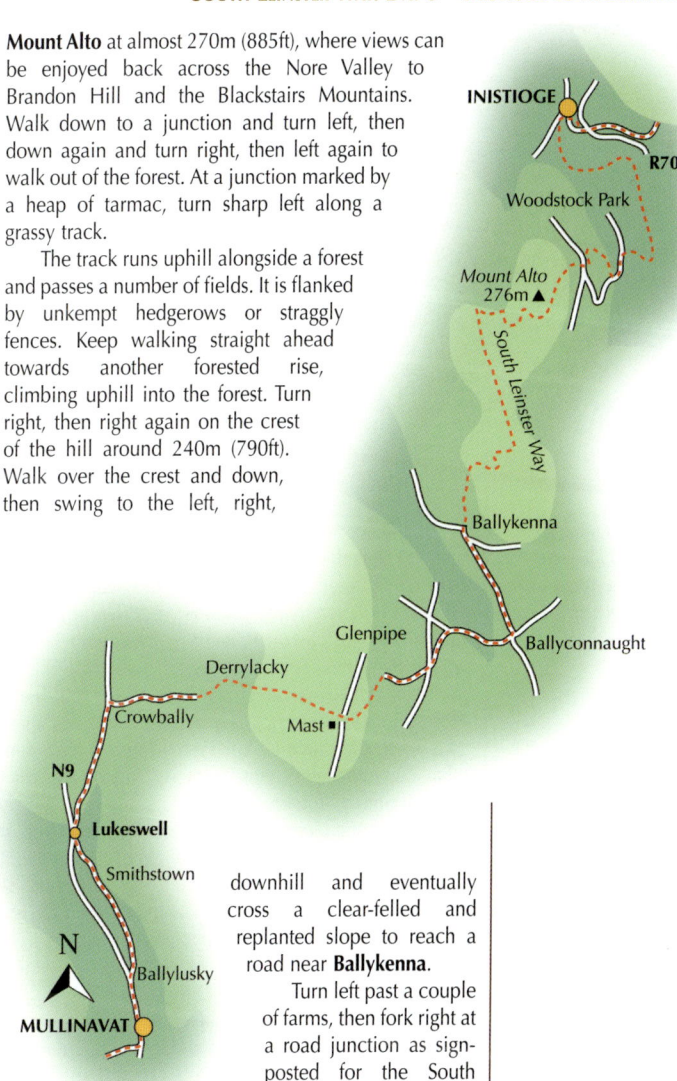

Mount Alto at almost 270m (885ft), where views can be enjoyed back across the Nore Valley to Brandon Hill and the Blackstairs Mountains. Walk down to a junction and turn left, then down again and turn right, then left again to walk out of the forest. At a junction marked by a heap of tarmac, turn sharp left along a grassy track.

The track runs uphill alongside a forest and passes a number of fields. It is flanked by unkempt hedgerows or straggly fences. Keep walking straight ahead towards another forested rise, climbing uphill into the forest. Turn right, then right again on the crest of the hill around 240m (790ft). Walk over the crest and down, then swing to the left, right, downhill and eventually cross a clear-felled and replanted slope to reach a road near **Ballykenna**.

Turn left past a couple of farms, then fork right at a road junction as signposted for the South Leinster Way. Walk along

THE IRISH COAST TO COAST WALK

Following a track through the old Woodstock estate after leaving Inistioge

the road, down across a dip, then up to a crossroads. Turn right and walk downhill to cross a bridge over the **Arrigle River**. Walk into the little settlement of **Glenpipe**, where there is a huddle of farm buildings. Turn left up a rather muddy road to reach a crossroads. The South Leinster Way is signposted straight uphill for distant Carrick-on-Suir. Walk up the road and follow it as it levels out beside a forest. Turn left along a grassy ride, then right along and up a track. Keep right to reach a road near a house and a tall communication mast. Turn right along the road, then left onto a broad forest track.

Keep to the clearest track climbing gently uphill on the forested slope. Cross the crest at almost 250m (820ft) and walk downhill through the area known as **Derrylacky**. Avoid other tracks heading off the right and left, and the main track eventually runs through the clear-felled and replanted lower slopes. Continue straight down a narrow road and cross **Derrylacky River**. Turn left at a road junction and eventually drop down to the busy N9 road at **Lukeswell**. Turn left and follow the road with care past Reade's Bar. Turn left up a narrow road past a B&B, in preference to the main road. Follow the narrow, quiet, undulating road and turn right downhill when a junction is reached marked by a cross. The cross records a mission that was once held in the parish. Follow the road under a railway, then turn left and walk with care along another stretch of the busy N9. The road leads straight into the long and straggly village of **Mullinavat**.

MULLINAVAT

Looking along the main street in the straggly village of Mullinavat

Accommodation in Mullinavat includes only a hotel and B&B, so it might be a good idea to book in advance. There is a post office, a few shops, several pubs and a couple of restaurants. Daily long-haul Bus Éireann services pass frequently through Mullinavat, with table number 4 linking with Dublin and Waterford, and table number 73 linking with Waterford and Athlone. There is a railway line through the village, but no railway station.

The Irish Coast to Coast Walk

DAY 10
Mullinavat to Carrick-on-Suir

Start	Mullinavat (grid ref 564247)
Finish	Carrick-on-Suir (grid ref 404216)
Distance	23km (14.25 miles)
Cumulative Distance	253km (157 miles)
Maps	OSI Discovery 75 & 76
Terrain	Road-walking throughout the day, first through low hills with a little forest, followed by more level cultivated countryside.
Refreshments	Piltown has a shop and pub

This day's walk is all along roads, though at least they are quiet for the most part, and in clear weather there may be good views across country towards the higher mountains. There is a chance to leave the road above Mullinavat to admire the lovely Poulanassy Waterfall set in a wooded valley. Although most of the road junctions are waymarked, and some are additionally sign-posted as the South Leinster Way, there are junctions where markers are missing, so keep an eye on the route description and map. The village of Piltown occurs part-way through the day, while Carrick-on-Suir marks the end of the South Leinster Way and beginning of the East Munster Way.

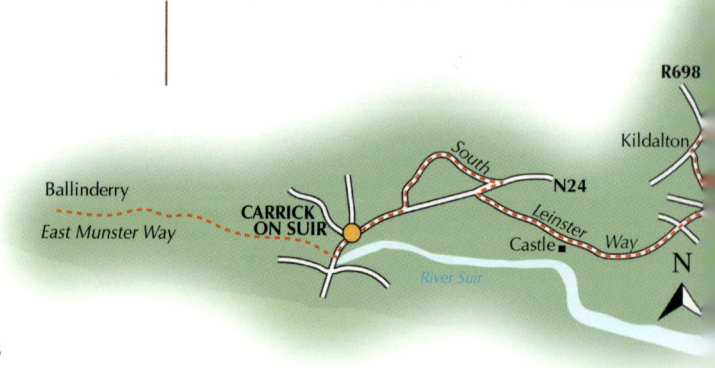

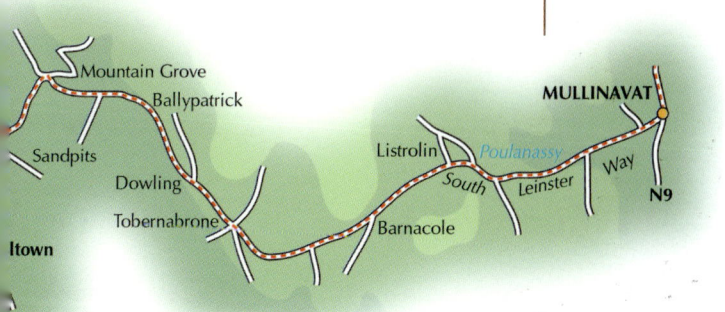

SOUTH LEINSTER WAY: DAY 10 – MULLINAVAT TO CARRICK-ON-SUIR

Walk along the busy Main Street, or N9 road, through **Mullinavat** and turn right as signposted for Piltown and the South Leinster Way. Cross the **Derrylacky River** and keep straight on as signposted for Piltown and Poulanassy Waterfall. Cross the **Poulanassy River** and follow the road uphill, keeping straight ahead at the next junction. The road runs over a rise and down into a dip. **Poulanassy Waterfall** is signposted down to the right, accessed along a broad, lawn-like path, and is obviously highly regarded locally. Water pours over a hard gritstone lip into a pool sheltered by trees.

Continue walking up the road in stages, bending right as signposted for Piltown, then heading straight through the next junction. Look back across country to the distant Blackstairs Mountains from a rise around 170m (560ft) near **Listrolin**. Walk downhill and keep straight ahead at all junctions, first keeping a patch of forest on the left, then later more forest on the right, around **Barnacole**. Turn right at a sort of crossroads, up a road signposted for Piltown. Views from the top of the road at **Barrabehy** stretch ahead to the Comeragh Mountains. Walk downhill through two minor crossroads, then uphill for more views from a road bend around 150m (490ft). Walk down through another crossroads at **Tobernabrone** and

89

The Irish Coast to Coast Walk

Poulanassy Waterfall lies just off the road shortly after leaving Mullinavat

SOUTH LEINSTER WAY: DAY 10 – MULLINAVAT TO CARRICK-ON-SUIR

keep walking straight ahead to reach a fork in the road. Bear left as signposted for Piltown.

Follow the road downhill and enjoy views of the Comeragh Mountains and rounded Slievenamon. At the next junction, avoid the road signposted for Piltown and turn right uphill instead at **Ballypatrick**. When the road runs downhill, keep left at the next two junctions and walk along a road flanked by woodlands at **Mountain Grove**. Keep straight on at a junction, but note the fine old gateways beside the road. Turn left at the next junction at **Jamestown**. Walk straight onwards through all other junctions, so that the wider and busier R698 road is followed past the prominent gateway of **Kildalton College** (an agricultural college). The road runs straight into **Piltown**, where there is a shop and bar at a junction with a main road. There is a little accommodation in the area if anyone wishes to break early, as well as buses onwards to nearby Carrick-on-Suir.

Turn right at the junction, then left at another junction beside a little stream spanned by a small stone bridge. This makes a useful picnic site if required. The road leads across the busy N24 by-pass, then becomes

Pleasant pastoral countryside stretches away to the Comeragh Mountains

THE IRISH COAST TO COAST WALK

little more than a narrow farm road. A sign on the left points out an old graveyard, while also on the left later is **Tibberaghny Castle**, surrounded by farm buildings. The castle can be visited on weekdays in the summer. Towards the end of the road on the left is the Carrick-on-Suir Rugby Football Club.

The busy N24 road is reached at **Three Bridges** and the course of the South Leinster Way has not been waymarked since the road was last altered. Turn right and walk up beside the busy road, then turn left along a minor road, or maybe shorten things by climbing the grassy embankment between the two roads! Follow the minor road and later head left down to a ford and footbridge on the **Lingaun River**. Crossing the river takes you from Co Kilkenny to the South Riding of Co Tipperary. The road up the other side passes the Lingaun River Water Treatment Plant, passes Green Hill Village and reaches the N24 road again beside the Sean Kelly Sports Centre on the outskirts of **Carrick-on-Suir**. Sean Kelly was Ireland's most renowned sports cyclist.

Turn right to follow the busy road into Carrick, passing under a railway bridge. The **Town Park** is a fine

Ormonde Castle, by the river at Carrick-on-Suir, is well worth exploring

green space, and once you are walking near it, turn left along a short, quiet suburban road. Follow a path across the grassy Castle Park to reach **Ormonde Castle** beside the River Suir. Turning right to walk into the centre of Carrick you will realise that you are already following the next trail on the Coast to Coast Walk, which is the East Munster Way, but for the time being you should explore the town.

CARRICK-ON-SUIR

This is the biggest town reached on the Coast to Coast Walk since leaving Dublin. Originally known as *Carrickmagriffin*, the town was founded in the 13th century. The River Suir is tidal all the way through and the river was for a long time the main transport route. Norman influence in this part of Ireland was essentially along a corridor beside the river. Carrick Bridge, or the Old Bridge, was built under the terms of a charter granted in 1306, though the current structure dates from 1447. Until the middle of the 18th century it was the lowest crossing point on the river, so Carrick had immense strategic importance. Repairs were recorded in 1614, 1688, 1697, 1788 and 1804. The town's greatest feature is undoubtedly Ormonde Castle and its Tudor Manor. The structure dates from 1450, but it is essentially an Elizabethan mansion – one of the best preserved from that era in Ireland. There is enough around Carrick to keep anyone interested for a whole day. Look in the Heritage Centre, located in an old church off Main Street, for background history about the town.

Facilities in Carrick include a good range of accommodation options, banks with ATMs, a post office, plenty of shops of all types, toilets and several pubs and restaurants. Bus Éireann services run frequently to several destinations, including table number 7 to Clonmel, Cork and Dublin. Table number 55 runs to Clonmel, Limerick and Waterford, as well as nearby Piltown and Kilsheelan. Table number 367 runs to Clonmel and Waterford, also taking in Piltown and Kilsheelan. The railway station offers trains to Rosslare Harbour, Waterford, Clonmel and Limerick. There is a Tourist Information Office in the Heritage Centre off Main Street (tel 051–640200).

STAGE 3
The East Munster Way

Walking beside a forest near Glenmoylan in the Knockmealdown Mountains (Day 13)

DAY 11
Carrick-on-Suir to Clonmel

Start	Carrick-on-Suir (grid ref 404216)
Finish	Clonmel (grid ref 208223)
Distance	30km (18.5 miles)
Cumulative Distance	283km (175.5 miles)
Map	OSI Discovery 75
Terrain	The first half of the walk is along a level riverside path, though this is overgrown in parts. The second half uses roads and tracks to climb a forested slope, ending back beside the river towards the end.
Refreshments	Pubs and a café at Kilsheelan. Powers the Pot is off-route near Harney's Cross Roads.

The East Munster Way starts easily and pleasantly along the banks of the River Suir at Carrick, but is a bit overgrown later. Beyond Kilsheelan, the riverside path could be followed onwards to Clonmel, but the waymarked route takes a more convoluted course. It zig-zags up a forested slope in the foothills of the Comeragh Mountains, only to descend to the river again and follow it into Clonmel at the end of the day. Clonmel is the biggest town yet reached on the Coast to Coast Walk, and as it falls roughly halfway across Ireland, with good connections to the rest of the country, it may be a good place to break the journey if you are covering the long trail in two trips.

Walkers follow the riverside path upstream on leaving Carrick-on-Suir

THE IRISH COAST TO COAST WALK

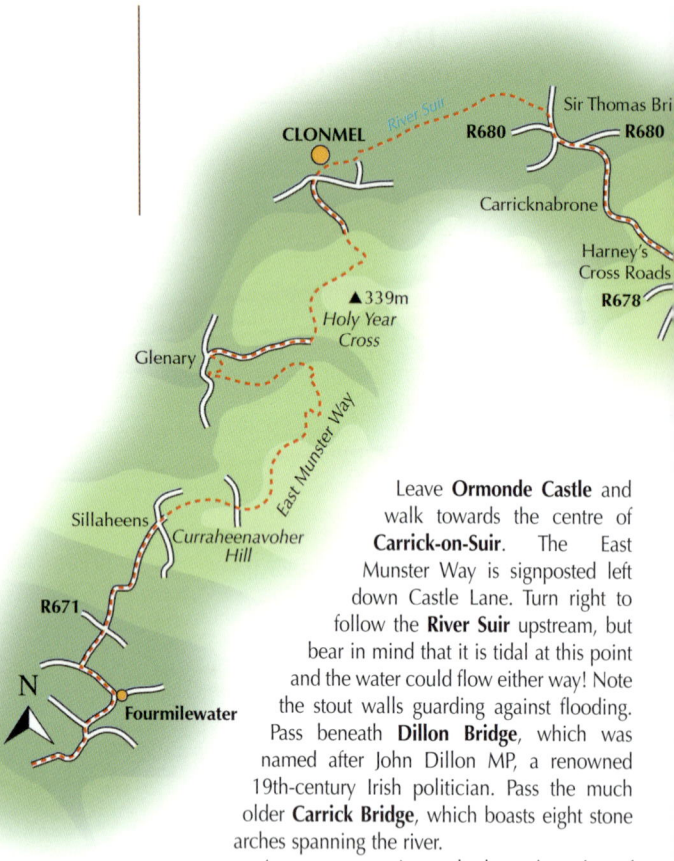

Leave **Ormonde Castle** and walk towards the centre of **Carrick-on-Suir**. The East Munster Way is signposted left down Castle Lane. Turn right to follow the **River Suir** upstream, but bear in mind that it is tidal at this point and the water could flow either way! Note the stout walls guarding against flooding. Pass beneath **Dillon Bridge**, which was named after John Dillon MP, a renowned 19th-century Irish politician. Pass the much older **Carrick Bridge**, which boasts eight stone arches spanning the river.

A green space is reached on the edge of Carrick, where a concrete riverside path continues upstream. The path passes the **Glanbia** works before the concrete runs out, while across the river a small round tower can be seen. A grassy path runs onwards, reaching a point where fishermen have vehicle access. The **Carrick-on-Suir Fishing Club** hut is passed and the grassy path remains in good condition for a while. When the fishing beat ends, however, the path is rougher and

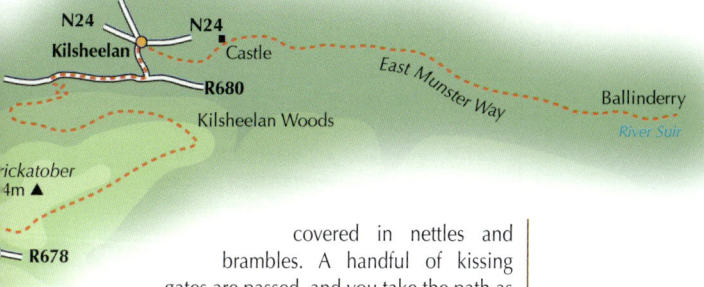

East Munster Way: Day 11 – Carrick-on-Suir to Clonmel

covered in nettles and brambles. A handful of kissing gates are passed, and you take the path as you find it. Look ahead to spot a tall tower-house overlooking a more pronounced bend on the river. A clear stretch of grassy path leads to the three-arched **Kilsheelan Bridge**, which boasts another small arch for the riverside path. You could follow the path upstream to Clonmel, but the East Munster Way actually crosses the bridge and takes a more circuitous course.

KILSHEELAN

Facilities in this straggly little village include a couple of B&Bs, a post office, a couple of shops, pubs and a café. Bus Éireann table numbers 7, 55 and 367 run to Carrick-on-Suir and Clonmel. Table number 7 runs also to Dublin and Cork, while table number 55 goes also to Waterford and Limerick, and table number 367 runs also to Waterford.

Cross **Kilsheelan Bridge**, from Co Tipperary to Co Waterford, and walk along and up a road to reach a junction. There is a memorial cross there to Count de la Poer, a Knight of Malta, who died in 1915 and whose family seat was at nearby Gurteen Castle. Turn sharp right and walk along a road flanked by walls and beech trees. Pass **Gurteen Cottage** and an access road for the castle. Follow the road onwards until a signposted left turn leads up a grassy forest track into **Kilsheelan Woods**. Turn right a short way up the track, following another bendy path or track to a higher level. Walk along a track beside a line

THE IRISH COAST TO COAST WALK

of beech trees at the top edge of a field. Turn right at a track junction, then almost immediately left. This track climbs and itself bends to the left. Turn left again at a junction with another track at around 170m (555ft). This track later falls gradually, and there are good views across country to the rounded form of Slievenamon.

When the track suddenly drops more steeply to the left, towards Kilsheelan, turn right up a lesser grassy track. Climb past a junction and follow the track until it levels out at another junction around 220m (720ft). Turn right up a stony track and keep left at a junction, then the track

Looking towards Knockanaffrin from a forest high on the East Munster Way

EAST MUNSTER WAY: DAY 11 – CARRICK-ON-SUIR TO CLONMEL

undulates straight ahead on the slopes of **Carrickatober** and there are views of the Comeragh Mountains from clearings. Bear right at a high junction, around 320m (1050ft), and walk straight downhill. Note the large standing stone of **Cloghadda** on the right, easily missed as tree branches are encroaching on it. Go through two gates to leave the forest and reach a road junction at **Harney's Cross Roads**. ▶

Turn right and follow the road downhill as signposted for the Munster Way. There are views of the Galty Mountains and Slieve Bloom, though these are lost as the road drops through a forest. Turn left as signposted at the bottom, then follow the road straight across **Sir Thomas Bridge** over the River Suir. This takes the route back from Co Waterford into Co Tipperary again. The old bridge has five stone arches for the river and one for the riverside path. Follow the riverside path upstream, which is later signposted as the popular **Riverside Walk** and is mostly surfaced at it enters **Clonmel**. When a busy road bridge is reached, the Waterford Road bridge, the East Munster Way crosses the River Suir, but if the town is to be explored it is best to head straight for the centre without crossing the bridge.

Not far off-route, on the road running uphill, is Powers the Pot, which offers a campsite, hostel and bar.

CLONMEL

This is the biggest and busiest town on the whole of the Irish Coast to Coast Walk. It also occurs somewhat short of halfway through the long trail, but makes a natural point to take a break if the route is being covered in two journeys. Clonmel is the administrative town for the South Riding of Co Tipperary and is basically an Anglo-Norman foundation like neighbouring Carrick-on-Suir. The town was walled in 1315 in response to the turmoil caused in Ireland by Edward Bruce. The town wall seen near Old St Mary's Church, however, dates from the 15th century, while the West Gate was built around 1830 on the site of an earlier gate. Cromwell beseiged Clonmel in 1650 and the town has housed a garrison force continually since that time. Kickham Barracks dates from 1780 and passed from British control in 1922. It was rebuilt in the 1940s. The County Museum offers more details on the history of the town. Charles Bianconi operated a transport system from

THE IRISH COAST TO COAST WALK

Clonmel from 1815. Today's traveller will find good bus and rail links, as well as a Museum of Transport.

Facilities around Clonmel include a good range of accommodation options, banks with ATMs, a post office, plenty of shops, toilets and several pubs and restaurants. Bus Éireann table number 7 runs to Dublin and Cork, as well as back to Kilsheelan and Carrick-on-Suir, and ahead to Clogheen. Table number 55 runs to Limerick, Kilsheelan, Carrick-on-Suir and Waterford. Table number 367 also runs to Waterford. Table number 368 and 388 run to Newcastle on Tuesday and Friday respectively. Table number 387 runs on Tuesday to Clogheen. Trains run to Limerick, Carrick-on-Suir, Waterford and Rosslare Harbour. There is a tourist information office (tel 052–22960).

Munster Way signpost near the busy town of Clonmel

DAY 12
Clonmel to Newcastle

Start	Clonmel (grid ref 208223)
Finish	Newcastle (grid ref 129135)
Distance	21km (13 miles)
Cumulative Distance	304km (188.5 miles)
Maps	OSI Discovery 74 & 75
Terrain	An easy walk from town is followed by a steep climb up a road into the hills. Paths, farm roads and forest tracks are followed by a longer road-walk through gentle pastoral countryside.
Refreshments	There is a pub at Fourmilewater.

The East Munster Way potters round the foothills of the Comeragh Mountains after leaving Clonmel. The punishingly steep Roaring Spring Road leads towards the Holy Year Cross high above town, then the route takes a circuitous course around Glenary. Zig-zagging tracks through Russellstown Forest are followed by a maze of minor roads as the route works its way across the Nire Valley to the little village of Newcastle. Bear in mind that accommodation is sparsely scattered in the countryside between Clonmel and Fermoy, so it is wise to book all your beds in advance.

Cross the Waterford Road bridge to leave **Clonmel** and turn right into Denis Burke Park as signposted. This is a fairly small, grassy, wooded space beside the **River Suir**. Leave by way of a gate that is dedicated to a number of authors associated with the town. Walk along the road a short way, then enter another small green space beside the river, overlooking a weir known as **Lady Blessington's Bath**. Turn left at a road junction to head for the hills. The road to use is signposted as the Munster Way, just to the right of a pub called The Emigrant's Rest. Walk uphill to a junction of narrow roads and turn left up **Roaring**

THE IRISH COAST TO COAST WALK

Lady Blessington's Bath is on the River Suir, seen when leaving Clonmel

Spring Road, which is signposted for the Holy Year Cross. Sometimes there is indeed a roaring spring beside the road, especially after heavy rain. Walking up the road leads from Co Tipperary into Co Waterford, and the ascent is steep for most of its length, though it levels out at a high corner. Follow a track up through a gate and out onto a slope covered in rhododendron. The **Holy Year Cross** is further uphill and can be visited for the fine views over Clonmel and the surrounding countryside.

HOLY YEAR CROSS

The East Munster Way used to climb all the way to the Holy Year Cross, but now it is omitted from the waymarked route. Clonmel, the Galty Mountains and rounded Slievenamon are prominently in view from the cross, which was erected in 1950. The surrounding Stations of the Cross were added in 1953. The structure is maintained by people living on the south bank of the River Suir at Clonmel. Thousands of worshippers climb up to the cross to hear Mass on the August Bank Holiday Monday each year.

EAST MUNSTER WAY: DAY 12 – CLONMEL TO NEWCASTLE

The waymarked route stays on the track, close to a fence around 300m (985ft), and eventually crosses the fence using a stile. Head straight towards a forest on **Cannon Hill**, then turn left and walk downhill beside it. A grassy track continues down to a farm in **Glenary**. Turn right to follow a narrow road away from the farm, enjoying views of the Knockmealdown Mountains in the distance. Eventually, a junction is reached with another road. Turn left, then left again, as signposted for the Munster Way along a forest track. There is a picnic site off to the left, but follow the track down into the forested glen. Bend to the right, then left along a bit of road to cross a bridge over **Glenary River**.

Turn left again after crossing the bridge to follow another forest track. This runs roughly parallel to the river and heads upstream. There is a glimpse of a curious ruin that could be reached by fording the river. This is known as **Carey's Castle** and was built in the 18th century as a residence. The track climbs through **Russellstown Forest**, followed by a right and left turn uphill. Keep straight on at a higher junction, then the track bends to the right and there is a view back towards Slievenamon. Turn right at an even higher junction where clear-felling has opened up views of the Knockmealdown Mountains, Galty Mountains and distant Slieve Bloom. The altitude is around 320m (1050ft). Follow the clear track gradually downhill, and go straight ahead at a junction and later cross a road at **Curraheenavoher Hill**.

The Munster Way is signposted down another forest track. Turn right at a junction of tracks and walk to another road. Turn left, then right as signposted again for the Munster Way. Walk down the road and keep left at a junction. Walk down through a crossroads as signposted for the Munster Way and Fourmilewater Church. At the bottom, turn left as signposted for the church. When the tiny village of **Fourmilewater** is reached, turn right as signposted along another road. Turn left at a house called Glasha and cross **Creggane Bridge** over the River Nire. Turn right to pass a pub called Lonergans, then turn right again at the next road junction, heading out of

103

THE IRISH COAST TO COAST WALK

Looking across fields in the Nire Valley towards the Comeragh Mountains

Co Waterford and back into Co Tipperary. Follow the road as it rises and falls across the valley side. Turn steeply down to the right at another junction, then at the bottom, turn left and walk straight towards the little village of **Newcastle**.

NEWCASTLE

Facilities at Newcastle are limited to a post office, a couple of shops and a pub. The nearest farmhouse B&B is off-route at Kilmaneen. Either walk there if accommodation is required, or call for a lift from the village. Bus Éireann table number 386 links Newcastle with Clonmel on Tuesday, while table number 388 does the same on Friday. Walkers who wish to continue to Clogheen the same day as leaving Clonmel are warned that it is a long way.

DAY 13
Newcastle to Clogheen

Start	Newcastle (grid ref 129135)
Finish	Clogheen (grid ref 003137)
Distance	22km (13.5 miles)
Cumulative Distance	326km (202 miles)
Map	OSI Discovery 74
Terrain	Minor roads at first, followed by a series of forest tracks.
Refreshments	There is nothing between Newcastle and Clogheen, though there is a small shop off the route at Goatenbridge.

The East Munster Way leaves Newcastle and picks its way across the northern slopes of the Knockmealdown Mountains. Minor roads give way to forest tracks, and there are fine views of nearby mountain ranges from clear-felled slopes. The latter part of the day's walk runs concurrent with a new trail called the Tipperary Heritage Way, so don't worry too much if this is the only trail actually named on signposts. The East Munster Way used to finish on the scenic R668, or 'Vee' road in the Knockmealdown Mountains, but it has been taken down to the village of Clogheen where it now links with the Blackwater Way. Walkers could of course cut out a lengthy loop at this point.

Follow the East Munster Way out of **Newcastle**, as signposted, up a road called **Bothar na nGall**. This is a delightful old road; battered, mucky and grass-grown. It climbs and bends right near the site of an ancient chapel, then eventually descends to a road junction. Turn left along the road and cross a bridge over **Glenboy River**. Swing left to follow the road uphill, pulling away from the river, until the road briefly levels out on a bend. Turn right here to cross a breeze-block stile and follow a winding, overgrown, brambly, grassy track uphill. Cross a couple

The Irish Coast to Coast Walk

of stiles and turn left up a clearer grassy track to reach the corner of a forest around 310m (1015ft). Turn right and follow the forest fence downhill towards the rounded, forested hump of **Knockroe**. Turn left to cross a stile and walk down to a forest track. Turn left along and down the track, passing the **Liam Lynch Monument**. This is in the shape of a round tower and commemorates a notable Republican volunteer who was shot by Free State forces in 1923.

Continue down the clear forest track, bending to the right and left, with views of the Comeragh Mountains and Galty Mountains from the clear-felled slopes. Walk down past all the junctions with other tracks to reach a sign-posted junction with the Munster Way and Tipperary Heritage Way. ◄

A right turn at this point leads to Goatenbridge and its little shop if supplies are needed.

Walk straight onwards from the junction to reach a gate and stile, with a signpost for the Munster Way and The Vee. The track crosses a bridge over **Glengalla River**, which drains from the highest Knockmealdown summits.

East Munster Way: Day 13 – Newcastle to Clogheen

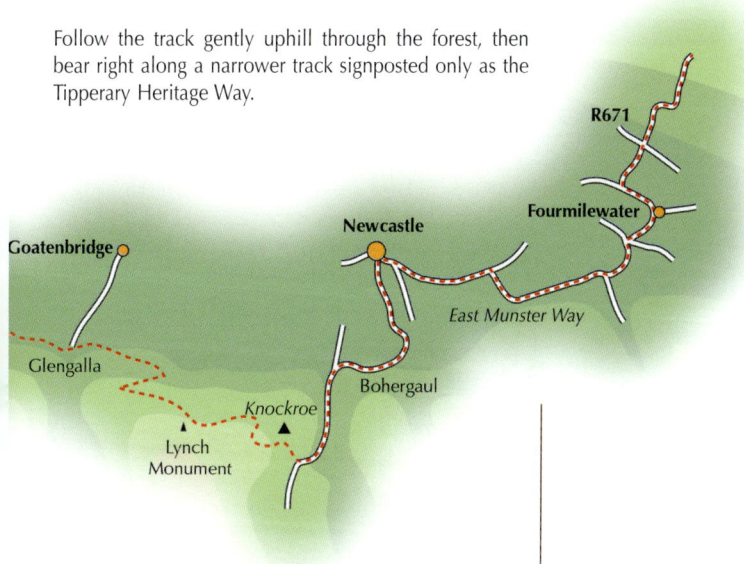

Follow the track gently uphill through the forest, then bear right along a narrower track signposted only as the Tipperary Heritage Way.

The track is narrower and more vegetated that the previous tracks, and can be wet and muddy in places. It later bends right downhill, then there is a left turn along another narrow track. Follow this onwards and it descends gently to ford a stream. Climb uphill and bend left, towards the mountains, on a slope of gorse and young forest. There are views across to the Galty Mountains and back to Slievenamon and the Comeragh Mountains. Walk straight through an intersection of tracks, rising ever so gently, passing a sign pointing off-route to the **Forrester's Hut**. Turn left up towards the mountains along another track as signposted. When the track bends left, walk instead to the right, crossing a stile and then a footbridge over a stream in **Glenmoylan**. Climb up a slope of bracken, gorse and heather, following a rough and stony path marked by posts. Head for a bend known as **The Vee** on a high stretch of mountain road at 250m (820ft).

The Irish Coast to Coast Walk

THE VEE

The Vee is a sharp bend on the R668 road that passes through the Knockmealdown Mountains. It offers a fine view of the broad and verdant vale between these mountains and the Galty Mountains, with the Comeragh Mountains and Slievenamon also seen. The low-lying land is largely used for grazing dairy cattle. Walkers can head down the road to Clogheen, or by glancing at the map, will spot an opportunity to head straight for The Gap and pick up the course of the Blackwater Way. However, this would mean committing yourself to a long walk at least as far as Araglin.

The East Munster Way runs concurrent with the Tipperary Heritage Way

EAST MUNSTER WAY: DAY 13 – NEWCASTLE TO CLOGHEEN

Looking at the Sugarloaf in the Knockmealdown Mountains from Clogheen

Follow the R668 road downhill from **The Vee**, enjoying views until the road is flanked by attractive pines and rhododendron. The road later bends well to the left and then, just before reaching a bridge, you should turn sharp right down a forest path. The path broadens and continues downhill as a track. Watch out for another waymarked path on the left, which narrows and fords a stream in **Glenlough**. Step up to a road and turn right, then turn left up a forest track. Turn right downhill from a junction, passing more pines and rhododendron to reach a lower road. Turn left as signposted for the Munster Way, all the way along the road to a junction bristling with signposts. Turn right to cross the **River Duag** and follow a road on the right into the village of **Clogheen**.

CLOGHEEN

Accommodation in the village includes only one B&B, but there is a farmhouse B&B and a campsite not too far away. Other facilities include a bank, post office, shops, pubs, a restaurant and a take-away. Bus Éireann table number 7 links Clogheen with Fermoy, Cork, Clonmel, Carrick-on-Suir and Kilkenny. Table number 387 runs on Tuesday to Clonmel.

STAGE 4
The Blackwater (Avondhu) Way

The 13th-century Ballyhooly Castle perched above the River Blackwater (Day 16)

DAY 14
Clogheen to Araglin

Start	Clogheen (grid ref 003137)
Finish	Barnahown, Araglin (grid ref 940079)
Distance	20km (12.5 miles)
Cumulative Distance	346km (214.5 miles)
Map	OSI Discovery 74
Terrain	Roads and forest tracks give way to hill paths and bog roads over exposed moorlands. The route later drops down onto quiet country roads.
Refreshments	There is nothing between Clogheen and Araglin. The farmhouse B&B at Barnahown offers snacks, while a pub and shop lie off-route at Araglin.

The Blackwater Way was originally developed as two trails: the Avondhu Way and Duhallow Way. Together they stretch all the way across Co Cork to Co Kerry. The first part of the route climbs high in the Knockmealdown Mountains after leaving Clogheen, then gradually drops to lower farmlands in the Araglin Valley. Walkers should bear in mind that there is only one farmhouse offering accommodation in the valley, and very little else before Fermoy, so be sure to book a bed unless walking the whole way. There are other stretches of the Blackwater Way where accommodation is sparse, and it may be necessary to arrange in advance a series of pick-ups and drop-offs along the way.

Leave **Clogheen** as signposted along Chapel Lane, which turns right. Turn left at a junction with the R668 'Vee' road as signposted across the **River Duag**. Follow the road away from the village, passing a hospital and **school**, then watch for a broad area of gravel on the right. A forest track heads straight towards the Knockmealdown Mountains, but swings left as it climbs at **Kilballyboy**, with masses of rhododendron to one side and views

THE IRISH COAST TO COAST WALK

across country to the Galty Mountains. Keep following the clearest track onwards, climbing a little, then dropping a little before turning round to the right and climbing again. The track becomes grassy underfoot and is flanked by pines and dense rhododendron. When the track suddenly swings sharp right, keep straight on instead along a narrower track. This leaves the forest and a clear path continues past **Bay Lough**. Masses of rhododendron clothe the slopes above the lovely little lake. The path rises to a car park beside the R668 road on **The Gap**, around 340m (1115ft).

There are two curious structures; one on either side of The Gap. To the left is a barrel-vaulted shelter that was once used by Bianconi Coach Services. To the right is a small **shrine** on the mountainside. To continue along the Blackwater Way, look for a gap in the roadside embankment just beyond the shrine. Follow the route as marked up a heathery, stony slope, then climb a very rough and stony path to the top corner of a forest. Turn left along the top edge of the forest, then drop downhill a short way. Turn right up a fine track, away from the forest, climbing up the slopes of **Knockalougha**. The track is grassy and well-buttressed. There is a bendy stretch, then it becomes

Knockmealdown Mountains seen above fields and woods at Clogheen

BLACKWATER (AVONDHU) WAY: DAY 14 – CLOGHEEN TO ARAGLIN

stony as it runs up to a gate at the corner of another forest. Don't go through the gate, but follow the route as marked along a fence crossing the high moorland slopes around 550m (1800ft).

The fence leads to another gate where a right turn leads along a grassy track. There is a forest on the left and heather moorland rising to the right. Turn left around a corner of the forest and walk down to a gate and ladder stile at another corner. Day-glo orange marker posts show the route of the Blackwater Way up a rugged moorland slope to around 600m (1970ft) on **Knockclugga**. Views stretch back along the heathery crest of the Knockmealdown Mountains to the rounded hump of Slivenamon. A short and fairly easy detour could include the sprawling cairn at 652m (2153ft) on **Knockshanahullion**, which is a splendid viewpoint.

Walk straight across a moorland shoulder, with views of the distant Galty Mountains, and turn left as marked along a stony bog road. This track is very bendy, but cuts a clear line down open slopes of grass and heather to reach a road at **Hare's Cross**. Turn left up the road, just to the corner of a forest, then turn right through a gate onto a moorland track. Follow the track and keep left at a fork as if heading towards **Crow Hill**. Cross a ladder stile at a gate and walk straight uphill, then keep right at a fork to cross a gap in the hills around 480m (1575ft). Keep left, then right, on the way downhill. The path to follow is in a rough and stony groove that bends in places. Watch carefully for a left turn and walk down a heathery spur bearing only a narrow path, though this becomes a rugged track later. It swings right and runs roughly parallel to the edge of some fields above **Doon**.

Cross a stile beside a gate and continue along a grassy track flanked by gorse. A clearer, stony track runs onwards to a road. Walk straight up the road and watch for another view of the Galty Mountains across a gap at **Knockeennanooneen**. The road runs into a forest and a left turn leads down a track to the bottom of the forest. Turn right along another road, and walk up through a peculiarly shaped crossroads. Turn left at a 'Yield Right of

THE IRISH COAST TO COAST WALK

The crest of the Knockmealdown Mountains seen from Knockshanahullion

Way' sign, then turn right at a junction to follow a narrow road at **Barnahown**. A farmhouse on the right offers accommodation and snacks to passing walkers. A farming museum is being developed across the road. The only other facilities nearby are a shop and pub off-route at **Araglin**. Think twice before passing this point as further facilities are a long way away.

DAY 15
Araglin to Fermoy

Start	Barnahown, Araglin (grid ref 940079)
Finish	Fermoy Bridge, Fermoy (grid ref 812985)
Distance	27km (17 miles)
Cumulative Distance	373km (231.5 miles)
Maps	OSI Discovery 74 & 81
Terrain	Roads, farm tracks and forest tracks through rolling countryside, ending mostly along roads
Refreshments	Pub at Mountain Barracks. Kilworth has a couple of shops and pubs.

The Blackwater (Avondhu) Way wanders through rolling countryside, following quiet country roads and farm tracks, with a few forests along the way. While the route is fairly straight forward, there are a lot of fiddly junctions of roads, tracks and paths that need care. Mountain Barracks is little more than a crossroads with a pub, and is followed by a long road walk. There is a moment, entering a forest from Keane's Cross, when it seems you may have strayed into an army firing range, but follow the waymarked route carefully and all will be well. Roads are followed from the village of Kilworth to the busy little town of Fermoy.

Continue along the road from **Barnahown**, which turns right and left uphill. Turn left downhill at the next junction, then right along another road. When this road swings right, watch for a left turn along a track. Go through a gate and follow the track until it runs down to a junction. Turn right at the bottom and pass a farm, then when the farm road swings left, keep straight ahead instead along a narrow, grassy track between vegetated walls. Turn right up a road, then left along a track. Follow the track to a junction at a farm. Turn right, then promptly left and pass through a forested area. The track reaches

The Irish Coast to Coast Walk

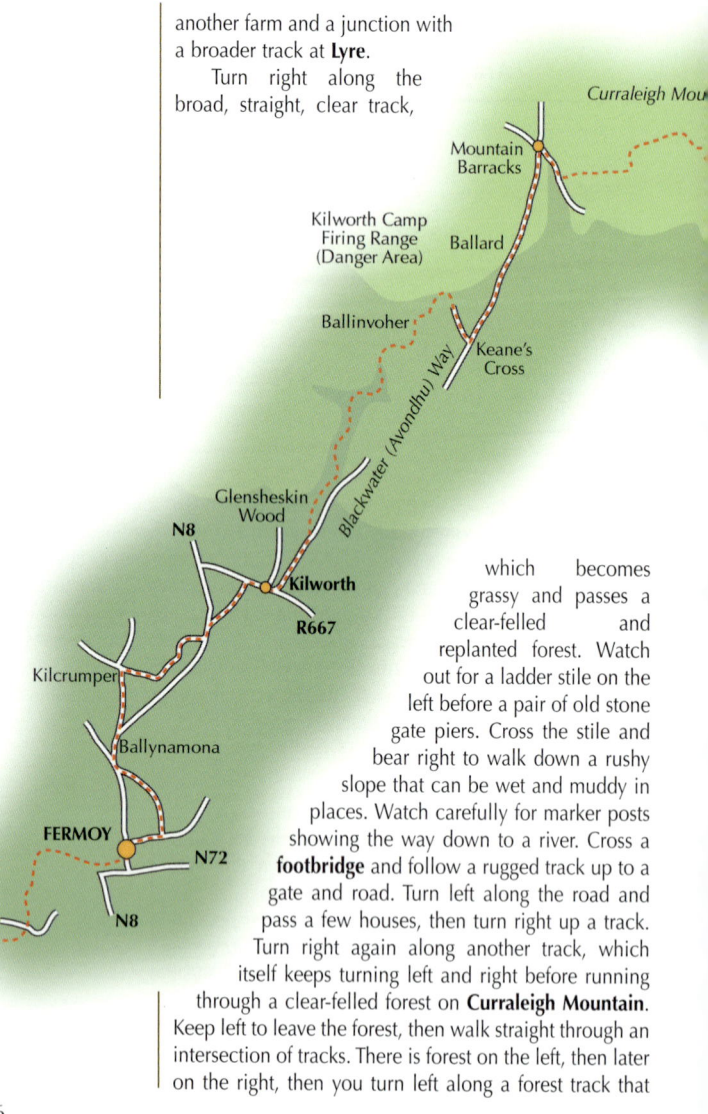

another farm and a junction with a broader track at **Lyre**.

Turn right along the broad, straight, clear track, which becomes grassy and passes a clear-felled and replanted forest. Watch out for a ladder stile on the left before a pair of old stone gate piers. Cross the stile and bear right to walk down a rushy slope that can be wet and muddy in places. Watch carefully for marker posts showing the way down to a river. Cross a **footbridge** and follow a rugged track up to a gate and road. Turn left along the road and pass a few houses, then turn right up a track. Turn right again along another track, which itself keeps turning left and right before running through a clear-felled forest on **Curraleigh Mountain**. Keep left to leave the forest, then walk straight through an intersection of tracks. There is forest on the left, then later on the right, then you turn left along a forest track that

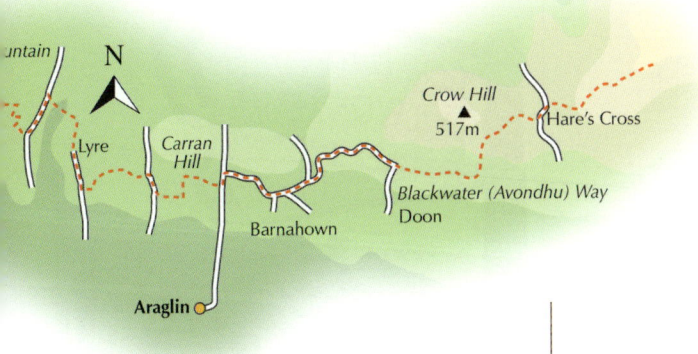

BLACKWATER (AVONDHU) WAY: DAY 15 – ARAGLIN TO FERMOY

later bends right. Walk straight out of the forest and follow a track downhill with fields alongside. At the bottom, turn right up the road to reach a crossroads at **Mountain Barracks**.

MOUNTAIN BARRACKS

Although the pub at the crossroads bears the name Mountain Barrack Inn, the barracks themselves were actually across the road. This was once the main Cork to Dublin highway and the barracks were built on a particularly remote stretch. The current main road, the busy N8, is some distance away and passes through Mitchelstown.

Turn left as signposted for Kilworth and Fermoy, and follow the road straight through a forest until **Keane's Cross** is reached. ▶ Turn right at the crossroads as signposted for Gorse Lodge. Walk to the end of the road and pass a barrier where a sternly worded notice warns of a firing range ahead. Follow the forest track downhill and be sure to turn left to avoid the range. Turn left again, then right, and follow the track down a forested valley at **Ballinvoher**. The track pulls away from the valley, so

This is a staggered crossroads with a B&B just beyond, if one is needed.

THE IRISH COAST TO COAST WALK

The Mountain Barrack Inn stands at a crossroads on an old coach road

watch for a path on the left dropping down through the trees. It is much wider by the time it reaches a lower forest track.

Turn left downstream alongside the **River Douglas**, enjoying a fine mix of trees along the way. Cross a bridge at a confluence of rivers and turn left through a broad gravel area. Continue walking downstream and there is later a footbridge on the left. Don't cross it, but stay on

BLACKWATER (AVONDHU) WAY: DAY 15 – ARAGLIN TO FERMOY

KILWORTH

Kilworth is an attractive little village with a pretty central green. Just off the green is the church which now serves as the Village Arts Centre. Facilities in Kilworth include an independent hostel, post office, a couple of shops and a few pubs. Bus Éireann table number 245 runs daily (except Sunday) to Mitchelstown, Fermoy and Cork. Nearby, out of sight, but not always out of earshot, is Kilworth Camp. Soldiers on the camp are trained on a series of firing ranges and there are warning notices should you draw close to the danger area.

the main track as marked. The track later crosses a bridge and passes through a wide grassy area with picnic tables. Cross over the river on another bridge and leave **Glensheskin Wood**. Walk straight ahead to follow a road uphill and away from **Glensheskin Bridge** and continue into the village of **Kilworth**.

Walk through the middle of **Kilworth** as signposted for Fermoy. ▶ Turn left as signposted for the Blackwater Way, leaving the village and walking down a road between tall and gloomy walls, with a glimpse of an old castle tower to the left. The busy N8 road is reached at the bottom. Cross this with great care and turn left to

An old milestone gives the distance to Dublin as 134 miles, but Coast to Coast walkers will have clocked at least 228 miles to this point!

The broad River Blackwater as seen from the main road bridge at Fermoy

The Irish Coast to Coast Walk

cross Downing Bridge over the **River Funshion**. Turn right at a gateway onto an old road now barred to traffic at this end.

Follow this old road onwards and go through a gate at its far end. Turn right along another road, then turn left at a crossroads to pass **Kilcrumper New Cemetery**. Walk through another crossroads to pass **Kilcrumper Old Cemetery**, reaching the busy N8 road again. Turn right along the road to reach a staggered crossroads on the outskirts of Fermoy. Turn left and cross the main road with great care. Follow a quiet road where there are views back to the hills on the left, while buildings are ranked all along the right. Turn right at the bottom of the road to follow another road parallel to the **River Blackwater**. Turn left to cross the busy Fermoy Bridge, which was rebuilt in 1865. The road leads straight into the centre of **Fermoy** by way of Pearse Square.

FERMOY

Fermoy traces it origins to the foundation of a Cistercian Abbey on the south side of the River Blackwater in 1170. A settlement grew around the abbey, but following the Dissolution, Fermoy did not enjoy much prosperity. The old abbey lands changed hands several times, then at the end of the 18th century a Scotsman called John Anderson bought the estate. He set up the Cork to Dublin mail-coach service and reorganised Fermoy. Large barracks were built early in the 19th century and Fermoy became a thriving garrison town. There was a railway through town from 1860 until closure in 1967.

The busy town has a good range of accommodation, both around town and in the nearby countryside, as well as a campsite. There are banks with ATMs, a post office, plenty of shops, toilets and several pubs and restaurants. Bus Éireann table number 7 serves Cork, Clogheen, Clonmel, Carrick-on-Suir and Kilkenny. Table number 8 serves Cork and Dublin, while table number 71 runs between Cork and Athlone. Table number 245 links Fermoy with Kilworth and Cork, while table numbers 242 and 366 offer only occasional links with Ballyhooley, Killavullen and Mallow. There is a tourist information office in a sports shop (tel 025–31101).

DAY 16
Fermoy to Killavullen

Start	Fermoy Bridge, Fermoy (grid ref 812985)
Finish	Killavullen (grid ref 648995)
Distance	26km (16 miles)
Cumulative Distance	399km (247.5 miles)
Maps	OSI Discovery 80 & 81
Terrain	A short riverside path gives way to a series of forest tracks and quiet country roads
Refreshments	Pubs and shop off-route in Ballyhooly

This is a fairly easy day's walk, starting with a short stretch of the River Blackwater at Fermoy. Forest tracks and minor roads rise and fall on the forested northern slopes of the Nagles Mountains, and a break can be taken just off-route in the charming little village of Ballyhooly. Forest tracks and roads, along with the occasional overgrown brambly path, lead onwards towards Killavullen. At the time of writing the village offered food and drink, but no accommodation, so ending there requires a pick-up to be arranged with other nearby accommodation providers. If fact, lodgings are sparse for several days, so plan ahead and make the necessary arrangements.

After crossing **Fermoy Bridge** turn right, as signposted for the Blackwater (Avondhu) Way, along Ashe Quay and the Barnane Walk which is beside the river. Pass Fermoy Rowing Club and later note **St Bernard's Well** on the left. The riverside path leads through fields and then along a path flanked by fencing and hedgerows (known locally as The Cage). The path was enclosed by a landowner wanting to screen off views of walkers, and includes a concrete tunnel! After another enclosed stretch, emerge from the fencing and turn right. When a road is reached, turn left as marked, then turn right, up an access track before reaching **Glenabo Bridge**.

THE IRISH COAST TO COAST WALK

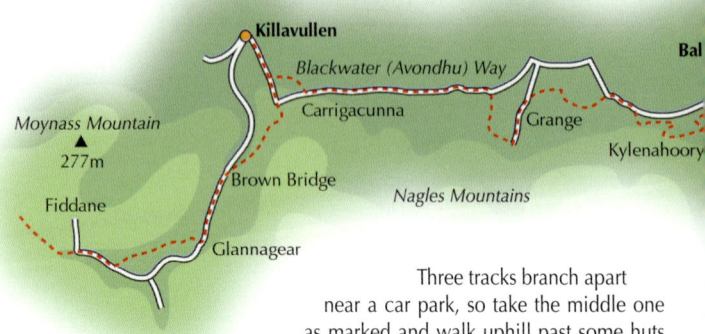

Three tracks branch apart near a car park, so take the middle one as marked and walk uphill past some huts and into a forest. Watch for a path rising to the right, then at the top step out onto a road and turn left. Follow the road uphill and out of the forest, winding past a few houses and farms. Turn left, as marked, along a track towards another forest and walk alongside it. Turn right along a good track leading into the forest. The track swings left and right on the slopes of **Knockananig**, then runs straight to a barrier at a junction. Turn left along another clear track enjoying views across country to the Ballyhoura Mountains across the Blackwater Valley.

When a yellow house is reached, turn right down another track. Walk down past a farm and continue down a road to a junction. Turn left down another road, then turn right at another junction to follow a narrow, bendy road down into a valley. Cross a bridge over the **Cregg Stream** and immediately turn left along a grassy track, passing a barrier. Walk upstream through woods, losing sight of the river. Climb to another barrier and turn right up a road, passing a house called The Highlands at **Ballynamuddagh**. Walk down to a crossroads and turn left. Follow the road until it enters a beech and conifer woodland at **Gurteen**. Turn right downhill, just inside the wood. A left turn reveals a vague path running parallel to the road, but some distance downhill from it. Turn right down a track, then left as marked at a junction beside a chestnut tree. The track can be muddy as it runs through the wood and down past a barrier. Ford a stream and turn right along a road to reach the **Bloomfield Crossroads** near **Ballyhooly**.

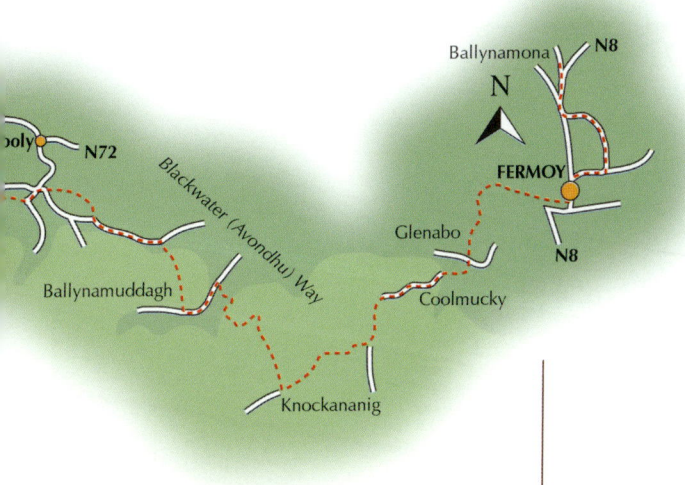

BALLYHOOLY

The lovely little village of Ballyhooly has a few points of interest. The *Book of Lismore* tells how St Carthage offered an apple to the local chieftain's daughter who suffered from a withered arm. As she took the apple, her arm was healed.

The castle overlooking the bridge was one of a string of castles along the River Blackwater – this one was built in 1314. It was held by Irish Royalists but fell to Cromwellian forces in the 17th century. There is an ancient graveyard near the Church of Ireland, tucked away beside the castle. At the top of the village is the old railway station site, comprising the former station master's house, the railway station itself and the old engine house.

Facilities in the village include a B&B (in the old engine house), post office, shop and a few little pubs. Bus Éireann table number 366 offers links with Fermoy, Killavullen and Mallow on Monday, Thursday and Saturday. Table number 242 does the same on Wednesday in summer.

THE IRISH COAST TO COAST WALK

Woodland track beside Cregg Stream on the Blackwater (Avondhu) Way

BLACKWATER (AVONDHU) WAY: DAY 16 – FERMOY TO KILLAVULLEN

Leave **Bloomfield Crossroads** by following the road uphill as signposted for Glenville. Turn right at a barrier and keep right along a forest track. This runs gently downhill among conifers, beech and chestnuts. Walk straight through an intersection of tracks and continue uphill. The track bends to the left, then you turn right to reach a dead-end. A brambly path is marked heading onwards, leading down to a farm road. Turn left uphill, past the green farm buildings, then the track turns up to the left. Turn right into a field, passing along the top edge. Watch carefully to spot a brambly step-stile on the left. Cross over and turn right through the brambly wood. Turn right down a grassy track to reach a junction, then turn left along another grassy track. There are occasional views across country stretching back to the Galty Mountains. When the track reaches a turning space, drop down to the right and proceed as marked to reach a minor road at **Kylenahoory**.

Cross over the road to avoid a bend, taking a sunken track down a wooded slope, then walk down the road. Turn left up a narrow road that quickly features a grassy strip up the middle. When the road descends, watch for a gate and stile on the right. An overgrown path between rampant hedgerows runs down to a forgotten little footbridge over a stream. Walk up another overgrown path to reach another gate and stile. Turn right along a much clearer grassy farm track. Turn left at **Grange**, down a battered road towards a forest. Fork right on entering the forest, then turn right along a track. This becomes nice and grassy, with views across the fields to the Ballyhoura and Galty Mountains. Follow the track, avoiding gates on either side, until it rises gently to a minor road.

Turn left along the road and follow it onwards, avoiding all junctions along the way. Watch on the right for a fleeting glimpse of **Carrigacunna Castle**. Further along the road turn right down a clear track, then left along a less clear track. This broadens later and you continue straight along a road to a junction. The waymarked route turns left uphill, but to visit **Killavullen** turn right downhill and walk straight into the village.

Ballyhooly Castle seen from the course of the Blackwater (Avondhu) Way

Blackwater (Avondhu) Way: Day 16 – Fermoy to Killavullen

KILLAVULLEN

This quiet village has no accommodation. A handful of big archways show that some of the houses once had stabling out the back for horses. Not far outside the village, in neighbouring Ballygriffin, Nano Nagle was born in 1718. She dedicated her later life to educating the poor, which carried great risk under the harsh Penal Laws. She founded the Presentation Sisters, shortly before her death, to continue her work. The Nano Nagle Centre was established in her memory at her birthplace in the village.

Killavullen has a post office, shop and a few pubs. Anyone breaking the journey at this point would need to call for a lift from nearby accommodation providers. Bus Éireann table number 366 offers links with Ballyhooly, Fermoy and Mallow on Monday, Thursday and Saturday. Table number 242 does the same on Wednesday in summer.

Walkers follow a woodland track near the village of Killavullen

The Irish Coast to Coast Walk

DAY 17
Killavullen to Bweeng

Start	Killavullen (grid ref 648995)
Finish	Bweeng (grid ref 500885)
Distance	33km (20.5 miles)
Cumulative Distance	432km (268 miles)
Map	OSI Discovery 80
Terrain	Forest tracks through low hills and minor roads through pastoral countryside. Some short paths may be overgrown by brambles.
Refreshments	There is nothing available on the route until Bweeng, though Mallow could be reached by a detour as it has many shops, pubs and restaurants.

Plan this day's walk in advance. There are no lodgings at either end of the route, and there are no shops or pubs along the way. However, the route does run fairly close to the bustling town of Mallow, and this does lend itself to splitting this long day's walk over two shorter days. If you cover the whole distance to Bweeng, you still need to organise a pick-up with a nearby accommodation provider as bus services are extremely limited. The first and shorter half of the day's walk links three forested areas together. The second, longer half is entirely along minor roads. There is an obvious way to short-cut the waymarked route, if desired, around Kilquane.

Leave **Killavullen** and retrace your steps back up the road. At the top corner of the road, by a gravel space at **Cappagh**, follow a track gently uphill. It is flanked by a fine assortment of trees and bushes. The track swings right, then further ahead at a fork, keep right to go steeply downhill among beech trees. Turn right towards the bottom to reach a parking space near **Brown Bridge**. Turn left and follow the road up through the forested **Glannagear** to find a parking space and **footbridge** on

BLACKWATER (AVONDHU) WAY: DAY 17 – KILLAVULLEN TO BWEENG

the right. Cross the bridge and climb uphill, then turn left along a gravel forest track. When this swings round to the right, leave it and continue straight along a grassy, brambly path. This runs broad and clear through a dense part of the forest. Keep straight ahead along another gravel track through a clear-felled area and descend to a road.

Turn right up the road and walk straight ahead to pass through a staggered crossroads. Turn left at a junction further uphill and follow another road straight past McCarthy's Meats depot. Follow a track straight up to a forest at **Fiddane**. Turn right inside the forest, head down a track, then keep right at a fork and descend further. Watch carefully on the right to spot brambly steps and a grooved, brambly path running downhill. This can be rather overgrown, but it leads out of the forest and down to a road beside a farm.

Turn right along the road, then left down the road to cross the **Fiddane Stream**. Walk uphill, along and gently downhill, keeping straight ahead at a junction. Later, watch for a track, flanked by trees, veering off to the left at **Knoppoge**. ▶ Follow the track and turn left as marked.

> Alternatively, follow the road onwards off-route to reach Mallow and a full range of shops, pubs, restaurants and accommodation options.

MALLOW

Although the busy town of Mallow is off-route, the scarcity of services on the route might lead you to visit the town at some point. Mallow was a notable spa town in the past, and it has a castle that was built in the 16th century. This is now a ruin, having been replaced by a more recently built castle which sits alongside the original's ruins. The castle grounds feature a unique herd of white fallow deer.

Facilities include a good range of accommodation, banks with ATMs, a post office, wide range of shops, toilets and plenty of pubs and restaurants. Bus Éireann table number 51 runs to Cork, Limerick and Galway. Table number 242 also runs to Cork, except Sunday, but also offers links with Bweeng on Friday, and Killavullen, Ballyhooly and Fermoy on Wednesday in summer. Table number 366 also serves Killavullen, Ballyhooly and Fermoy on Monday, Thursday and Saturday. Trains run to Cork and Dublin as well as ahead to Millstreet and Killarney.

The Irish Coast to Coast Walk

Bus Éireann table number 51 is an express service which may not stop. Table number 242 runs daily except Sunday and has an official stopping point at nearby **Mourneabbey Cross**.

Walk up to a gate to enter a forest, then turn right through a smaller gate. Follow a narrow path flanked by gorse bushes and brambles to reach a grassy forest track further uphill on the slopes of **Knockaroura**. Turn left up the track and follow it straight ahead, avoiding all other tracks to left and right, and descend gradually to a barrier and a road at **Carrigduff**.

Turn left along the road, then right; the road is so grass-grown and broken that it is more like a farm track. Turn left at a road junction and go across a dip in the road, passing a memorial cross to reach a busy main road at **Ballynamona**. This is the N20 road, which carries bus services offering occasional links with **Mallow** and Cork.

◀ Cross the busy N20 road with care and walk straight down a path through **Ballynamona**. An old church and cemetery are seen to the left, but turn right down a road, then left to go under a railway bridge. The Blackwater (Avondhu) Way is signposted down to the right, crossing **Ballynamona Bridge**. Turn left up another road, which levels out with a view of the crumbling ruin of **Castlebarrett**. Walk along and up the road, straight ahead at a junction, then left at the next junction at

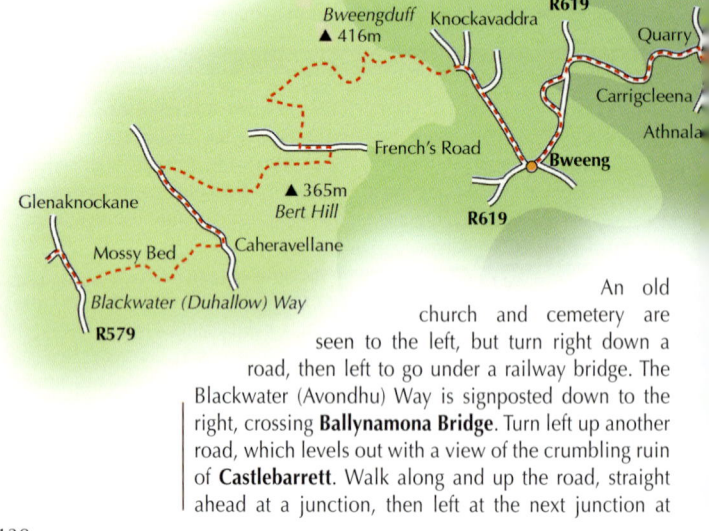

130

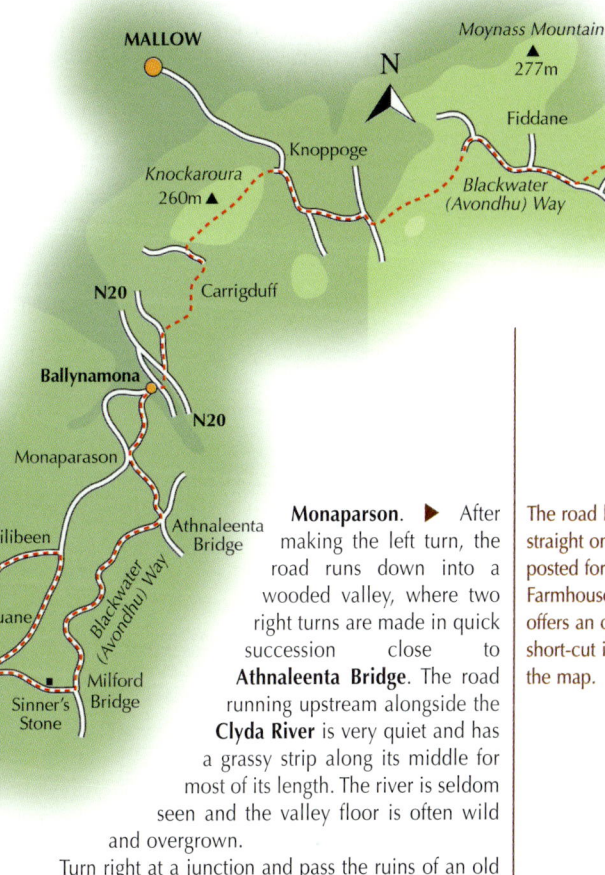

BLACKWATER (AVONDHU) WAY: DAY 17 – KILLAVULLEN TO BWEENG

Monaparson. ▶ After making the left turn, the road runs down into a wooded valley, where two right turns are made in quick succession close to **Athnaleenta Bridge**. The road running upstream alongside the **Clyda River** is very quiet and has a grassy strip along its middle for most of its length. The river is seldom seen and the valley floor is often wild and overgrown.

Turn right at a junction and pass the ruins of an old church. A curious lump of rock with a hole through it is known as the **Sinner's Stone** and stands across the road. Follow the road onwards and turn right at a junction beside **Athnalacka Bridge**. Follow the road uphill, along and gently downhill, passing houses and farms along the way at **Kilquane**. Turn left up a road, as marked at

The road leading straight on is sign-posted for Kilquane Farmhouse and offers an obvious short-cut if you study the map.

131

THE IRISH COAST TO COAST WALK

Ballyfilibeen, following it along and down into a broad dip to cross the **Shinagh Stream**. The road bends as it climbs through **Carrigcleena Beg**, then reaches a junction. Turn right and then, later, left to follow a road beside a quarry (this could be rather noisy).

The bendy road could be well manured in places on the way through **Carrigcleena More**. Keep straight on at a junction, then later turn left down the R619

The crumbling ruins of Castlebarrett are passed above Ballynamona

BLACKWATER (AVONDHU) WAY: DAY 17 – KILLAVULLEN TO BWEENG

A makeshift altar in a ruined church passed after following the Clyda River

road. The road has been straightened, but you can still use the old bend off to the right. Either way, reach the scattered village of **Bweeng** in an elevated situation at 220m (720ft).

BWEENG

Facilities at Bweeng are limited. There are no lodgings, so arrange a pick-up with a nearby accommodation provider. There are two pubs on the route through the village, and a post office shop off-route near the church. When the Blackwater Way was first established, it came in two halves: the Avondhu Way and the Duhallow Way. Bweeng is where both routes are joined together. Nearby Laharan Cross is famous for its outdoor crossroads dancing! Bus Éireann table number 242 is a Friday only link with Cork and Mallow.

STAGE 5
The Blackwater (Duhallow) Way

The Paps, once revered as a manifestation of the Celtic goddess Áine (Day 20)

DAY 18
Bweeng to Millstreet

Start	Bweeng (grid ref 500885)
Finish	Millstreet (grid ref 275890)
Distance	40km (25 miles)
Cumulative Distance	472km (293 miles)
Maps	OSI Discovery 79 & 80
Terrain	Mostly forest tracks and minor roads, with some bog roads and a couple of rather rugged forest rides and open moorland
Refreshments	There are none available along the route. Millstreet Country Park has a seasonal restaurant off-route.

This is a very long day's walk, and again there is no accommodation at the start, and none along the way until you reach Millstreet. There are no places offering food or drink on the route either. In fact, this is a particularly remote part of the Irish Coast to Coast Walk, as it makes a complete traverse of the empty Boggeragh Mountains, taking in extensive forests and broad boglands. If the route needs to be cut shorter, then arrange for a pick-up with a nearby accommodation provider, perhaps meeting at the Mushera car park, or by the gates of the Millstreet Country Park. Most of the final stage is along minor roads down to Millstreet and the distance can be covered quickly.

Leave **Bweeng** by taking the road signposted for the Blackwater (Duhallow) Way and Laharan Cross. There are views from this road stretching back across country to the distant Galty Mountains. Keep left at two road junctions (the latter signposted for Laharan Cross). Turn left at a barrier to walk up a forest track at **Knockavaddra**. Turn right at a junction and follow a track with telegraph poles alongside it. Pause at a left bend on a clear-felled slope, to look back across country to the Ballyhoura Mountains,

THE IRISH COAST TO COAST WALK

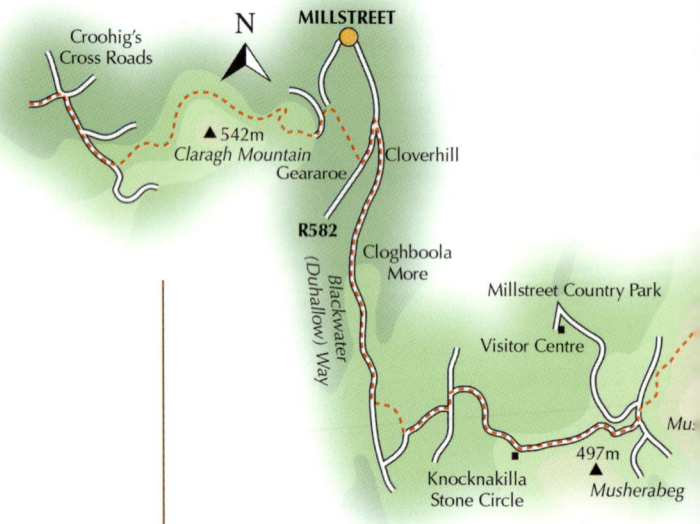

Galty Mountains and part of the Knockmealdown Mountains. Keep climbing and cross the shoulder of **Bweengduff** around 370m (1215ft). The track appears to lead up to a series of masts on top of the forested hill, and there is a view ahead to Musheramore and the Derrynasaggart Mountains. Turn left down a clear track, avoiding the masts, in the direction of those distant mountains. Walk straight past one junction, then turn left at the next at **Glanaharee East**. The track later turns right and runs up to **French's Road** at a barrier.

Turn left and walk gently up and down the road, then turn right into the forest. Follow a track uphill from a barrier, and keep to the track as it turns right. Simply follow the track onwards, gradually uphill to around 355m (1165ft), then down the slopes of **Bert Hill**. Keep straight ahead at a junction. A barrier and road are reached at a ruined cottage. Turn left along the road, which is battered and grass-grown, passing a little house and a tabular rock outcrop then crossing the **Caher River**.

Blackwater (Duhallow) Way: Day 18 – Bweeng to Millstreet

Walk up from the river and turn right past a barrier to follow another forest track. Turn left up through clear-felled and replanted forest to reach the end of the track. Walk ahead as marked, crossing tussocky grass along a forest ride. Take care crossing a hidden stream full of orange water. Walk up a sunken track between the forest and bog to reach a firm bog road. Turn right to follow this rugged track, passing most junctions until you turn left uphill as marked. The track becomes grassy, wet and boggy as it crosses the **Mossy Bed** around 350m (1150ft). Walk downhill and cross a bridge over a stream, then turn right and walk down the R579 road. ▶

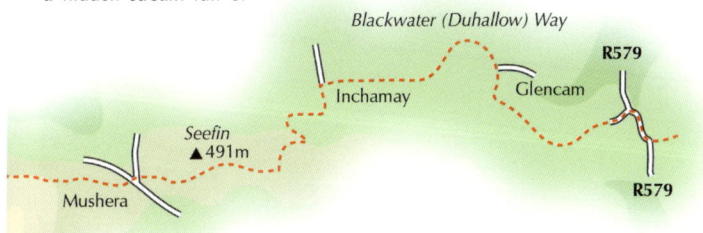

Turn left up a narrow road with a grassy strip up the middle. There are fields on either side and a view back to Bweengduff. The road runs through a bit of forest and out onto a broad, grassy, heathery bog. The way ahead is largely grass-covered and the road swings gradually across the slopes of a valley, around 360m (1180ft), then drops down to cross **Glencam River**. Walk uphill and go straight past a gate and ladder stile to follow a forest track. The forest has been clear-felled and replanted. Walk downhill and turn left at a junction, then walk downhill and turn left off a right-hand bend. Walk up a rugged forest ride, and keep right when a fork is reached. Cross a dip where there is a hidden stream, then walk up a slope of awkward, tussocky grass to reach the forest fence at **Inchamay**. Cross the fence and turn right to walk alongside it.

The moorland beside the forest is tussocky, then a hidden stream has to be crossed at the corner of the

This road leads off-route to the tiny village of Nad and larger village of Banteer. There is a pub at Nad and accommodation, food and drink at Banteer, but a long way off-route.

137

A rugged tract of moorland at Inchamay on the Blackwater (Duhallow) Way

forest. Climb up an awkward slope to reach a deeply entrenched bog road. This is rugged at first, but becomes much easier to follow later. Cross the **Ownagluggin River** and walk beside a bit of forest, then turn left along another track to cross the river again. Walk up the track and turn right to climb gently up a boggy slope. Turn left at a junction to climb towards a forest and look back towards the Ballyhoura Mountains, Galty Mountains, Bweengduff and a glimpse of the Knockmealdown Mountains.

The track leads up into the forest, then there is a sharp right turn along a grassier track. This track climbs gently to over 450m (1475ft) on the forested hill, then drops a little. Turn right along a short, narrow, tussocky forest ride. Cross a stile over a fence and look ahead across a grassy moorland to spot a narrow path and orange day-glo marker posts. A couple of these markers show the way onto an old bog road. Turn right up it, then drift downhill across the slopes of **Seefin**, from about 460m (1510ft). Head towards the bulky form of Musheramore to reach a car park and road junction. ◄ An old milestone gives distances to Millstreet and Cork,

This is a handy place to arrange a pick-up.

while a Blackwater (Duhallow) Way signpost points across the road.

A clear track climbs up a slope planted with young forest trees. When the track ends, continue following a line of orange day-glo marker posts across the grassy, heathery slopes of **Mushera**. Cross a stile over a fence and trace more marker posts across the slope, contouring around 500m (1640ft) on the steep slopes. Link with a grooved path running parallel to a forest, though some distance above the trees. There are views taking in Mullaghanish, Mangerton Mountain, The Paps, Caherbarnagh, Claragh Mountain, the rolling moors of North Cork, Slieve Bloom, Ballyhoura Mountains, Galty Mountains, Slievenamon, Knockmealdown Mountains, Bweengduff, Comeragh Mountains and Seefin. Seldom have views been so extensive!

Walk down the rough and stony grooved path to enter the forest, and keep heading down to follow a better track. When a gate and ladder stile are reached, the route turns left. ▶ Step over another ladder stile and ford a stream to leave the forest. The path is wet and muddy in places. Cross yet another ladder stile and head for a signpost at a road junction.

The Blackwater (Duhallow) Way is signposted from the road junction. As you follow the road, watch out for a rocky patch on the right which is known as **Carrig Leabra**. ▶ The road overlooks **Millstreet Country Park**, then later there is a kissing gate on the left and access to **Knocknakilla Stone Circle**. Follow the road onwards,

It is worth turning right and walking a short way to visit a pilgrimage site at St John's Well, where a grotto was built in the 1950s and then surrounded with the Stations of the Cross.

Carrig Leabra was a 'hedge school' site in penal times, and was used as a remote outdoor school by travelling teachers when Catholics were refused an education.

MILLSTREET COUNTRY PARK

The Millstreet Country Park is off-route, but can be reached using the stout gateway nearby. There are several marked nature trails around the site, which takes in 200 hectares (500 acres) of rugged moorland, forest and fields. Down in the valley there is a visitor centre and restaurant, with gardens to explore. Red deer are reared in a number of pens around the Country Park. If this long day's walk is split over two days, then there should be time to make a decent exploration of the site and enjoy its facilities.

THE IRISH COAST TO COAST WALK

The tall and tilted central pillar in the ancient Knocknakilla Stone Circle

BLACKWATER (DUHALLOW) WAY: DAY 18 – BWEENG TO MILLSTREET

though a forest and out the other side. The road passes some fake 'megaliths' planted around a field, though the **standing stone** inside the field is genuine. Turn left at a road junction, then right at the next junction. Walk along and down the road, then turn right up a narrow farm road at **Carrigacooleen**. At the first building, go through a gate on the left and follow a grassy track, undulating past fields to reach a gate and another minor road.

Turn right a short way up the road, then walk downhill, noting that this quiet lane is largely grass-grown in the middle. Claragh Mountain is prominent across the valley. Follow the gently rolling road, walking straight ahead at all junctions. It loses its grassy strip and descends through **Cloghboola More** and **Cloverhill** to reach a Marian grotto at a junction with the busy R582 road. The route turns left at this point, and the Geararoe B&B is just along the road. By turning right, however, and walking straight into **Millstreet** you can make use of the town's full range of facilities.

MILLSTREET

This busy little town is well known in equestrian circles for the Green Glens Arena and its show-jumping competitions. There are a few places offering accommodation around the town and in the nearby countryside, as well as banks with ATMs, a post office, plenty of shops, toilets, and a variety of pubs and restaurants. Bus Éireann services come through the town, with table number 40 offering regular links with Tralee, Killarney and Cork. A railway station is signposted some distance out of town, with services to Killarney, Cork and Dublin. An interesting museum is located in the Carnegie Hall, and there is a tourist information office in the same building (tel 029-70844).

The Irish Coast to Coast Walk

DAY 19
Millstreet to Shrone

Start	Millstreet (grid ref 275890)
Finish	Shrone (grid ref 134888)
Distance	22km (14 miles)
Cumulative Distance	494km (307 miles)
Map	OSI Discovery 79
Terrain	Paths can be rather rugged and vague at times across open hill and mountainsides, but the route is well-marked. Some of the later boglands are quite rugged and largely pathless, and more care is needed to spot markers.
Refreshments	None on the route

Accommodation and facilities remain absent throughout this day's walk, so again, book in advance and be sure to carry any supplies you need. The Blackwater Way takes an interesting course as it traverses the northern slopes of the Derrynasaggart Mountains, turning round Claragh Mountain, crossing the lower slopes of Caherbarnagh, and passing a couple of lonely little mountain lakes. The route finally leaves Co Cork and enters the 'Kingdom of Kerry' which is the last county visited on this long Coast to Coast Walk across Ireland. Broad boglands and a valley are crossed before the route reaches The City at the foot of The Paps in the scattered village of Shrone.

Follow the Macroom road, or R582 road, away from **Millstreet**, which is signposted from the Marian grotto as the course of the Blackwater (Duhallow) Way. Take care as the road is busy, and follow it across the **River Finnow**. Pass Geararoe B&B and turn right at an access for The Garden Fairies, where plants are sold at an old estate gatehouse. Pass clumps of rhododendrons and follow a grassy track to a gate and stile. Cross a field to reach another gate and stile, then continue up through a

BLACKWATER (DUHALLOW) WAY: DAY 19 – MILLSTREET TO SHRONE

Walkers crossing the heathery slopes of Claragh Mountain near Millstreet

wonderfully mixed patch of woodland. Pass the crumbling ruin of **Mountleader House** and enjoy a view back to Musheramore.

Walk straight ahead to pick up a grassy track leading to a pleasant pond. Turn left and cross a ladder stile, then walk up beside a field to reach a gate and road beside a woodland. Turn left up the road, walking alongside the wood, but watch carefully for a grassy track climbing to the right, up into the wood. It swings left and right as it climbs, then you cross a stile on the left. Walk along the edge of a forest, with gorse bushes alongside. There is another view back to Musheramore, while **Claragh Mountain** rises ahead. Turn right into the forest, wriggling right and left as the path runs down a slope, with the gorse pressing in closely. Turn a sharp right bend, then turn left down to a gate.

Go through the gate and follow a clear, grassy track up a steep slope, to reach the top edge of a forest. Walk alongside the forest, with views back to Millstreet, the Ballyhoura Mountains and Galty Mountains. Go through another gate and leave the far corner of the forest around 330m (1080ft). A few steps on the left lead up to a waymarked route along a narrow path across a heathery

143

THE IRISH COAST TO COAST WALK

slope. Views ahead take in Caherbarnagh, MacGillycuddy's Reeks and the mountains of the Dingle Peninsula. Cross a stile over a fence and forge through more heather and gorse scrub. Follow a path alongside a fence, roughly contouring across the rugged slopes, but also keep an eye open for marker posts. Cross a stile over another fence and find the way round a hollow on the mountainside before following a grassy, rushy track uphill. Cross another stile over a fence and walk down to a marker post. Walk down a grassy track and cross a little boulder-strewn valley. Walk to a gate, ladder stile and road. Turn right to walk down to **Croohig's Cross Roads**.

Turn left as signposted at the crossroads. ◀ The road crosses **Ahaphooca Bridge**, then you turn left up towards the mountains. Follow a narrow tarmac road until it suddenly turns left in front of a house. Keep to the right of the house and follow clear tracks uphill, as marked, through a series of gates. The higher parts can be muddy. Turn right at the top of the track to follow a narrow path through masses of gorse. Walk up a rugged moorland slope beside an electric fence at **Gortavehy East**, then turn right to cross it using a ladder stile. Follow the path uphill as marked, on a rugged moorland slope of tussocky grass, gorse and heather.

Cross a small stile over a fence, around 380m (1250ft), and let orange day-glo marker posts lead across an overgrazed bog where the path is vague or absent. Turn right along a clear, stony path and enjoy views of **Gortavehy Lough** on the way down a slope of gorse. Turn left at the bottom

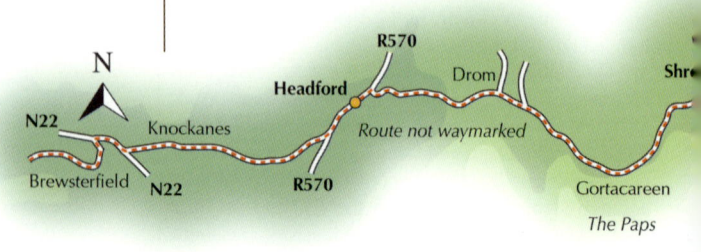

The village of Ballydaly, with its shop and pub, can be reached by walking straight ahead off-route.

144

as if approaching the lough, but turn right beforehand and cross another fence to continue. Contour across wet ground to reach firmer footing and look ahead to spot marker posts. Also, look back across the valley to spot the tumbled remains of an ancient stone fort, or 'rath'. There is no trodden path across a boulder-studded slope of short grass, and the marks of ancient enclosure walls can be discerned. The route follows a stony track beside a wall and fence that separate the lower fields from the open mountainside at around 300m (985ft). Cross an awkward little stream with care, then cross a little stile and follow a narrow path up a slope of gorse and heather to continue along a muddy trench. Look down to a farm to spot another rath alongside. Turn left and cross a stile over a fence, then follow another fence onwards across a boggy slope. **Lough Murtagh** is hidden in a hollow up to the left.

Cross a fence and follow a straggly fence onwards, up and across a rugged slope of heather. Look back to Claragh Mountain, and even as far as the distant Galty Mountains. Look ahead to The Paps, MacGillycuddy's Reeks and the mountains of the Dingle Peninsula. Forge across the rugged, heathery slopes, looking ahead to spot marker posts. The path runs uncomfortably close to a fence, but watch to spot where it rises away from the fence. The route is sparsely marked along a narrow and rugged path across the heathery slope, touching 400m (1310ft). Cross a broader path and walk gradually back towards the fence. Cross a stile over the fence and look across a grassy slope to spot a day-glo marker post.

A marker post at Awnaskirtawn points across bogs towards The Paps

Take care on the descent, crossing wet and slimy rocks, boggy patches dribbling with water, with cliffs above and below. Do not short-cut into the valley, but follow the marker posts faithfully, as if heading towards the top end of the valley. Notice the abundant growths of St Patrick's Cabbage (at least where the sheep cannot graze); a common saxifrage in the west of Ireland.

Swing sharp right at a fence, then walk down the valley to cross the stream and a fence as marked. Walk across the valley and up a slope of tussocky grass and bog myrtle, and cross a fence with no stile. Continue as marked across tussocky grass and heather to cross a small stile over another fence, around 300m (985ft). Head towards a forest at **Awnaskirtawn** and walk down alongside it. The ground is very rugged, with deep heather, tussocky grass and gorse bushes. Turn left across a stile and walk onwards as marked to cross another stile. Turn left along a muddy firebreak track alongside the forest. The twin peaks of The Paps begin to loom large from here and dominate the route for some time.

Cross a track and go through a gate. Cross a field and a stream in a valley and climb, as marked, along another firebreak track beside a young forest. Drift slightly right across barren, open bogland at **Shrone More**. As the slope drops gradually downhill there is no real path, so look out for marker posts leading to the edge of a forest. Cross a stile and turn right through a gate, then let a grassy ride lead onwards to a lower gate. Follow the route, as marked, through a bouldery field above a farm. Turn left over a ladder stile and walk down to a gate at the bottom of a field and onto a road. Go straight through another gate to leave the road and walk down a rugged slope, looking for markers to spot gaps in walls and bushes. The valley bottom is boggy and a little **footbridge** spans a river.

Cross the footbridge and turn right downstream as marked through bouldery ground. Later, turn left uphill to follow a rugged grassy track with gates. Walk down a well-manured track and turn left up another track as marked. This track, or battered road, climbs and swings right, then runs downhill a little. Look to the right to find The City, otherwise known as the ancient fort of **Cathair Craobh Dearg**.

CATHAIR CRAOBH DEARG

Cathair Craobh Dearg, the 'fort of the red claw' (or The City), has long been associated with fertility rites. Though it looks as though it may simply be a defensive prehistoric stone fort, its location is significant. It lies in the shadow of The Paps – two breast-like mountains crowned with nipple-cairns that were venerated as a manifestation in the landscape of the Celtic goddess Aine. Perhaps The City is the navel of the goddess. Cattle were once penned into the old fort in the hope of receiving protection from ailments. The place is now the venue for an annual Christian pilgrimage and there are several crosses carved on stones around the site, which includes a holy well.

Although there is a ladder stile and marker post on the left of the road, with **The Paps** dominating the landscape, the waymarked trail actually ends abruptly nearby. There is presently no waymarked link between the Blackwater Way and the Kerry Way to lead walkers from Coast to Coast, but a route has been suggested in recent years along a series of minor roads. So, stay on the road and walk downhill from The City. Cross a bridge and

THE IRISH COAST TO COAST WALK

Cathair Craobh Dearg, or The City, is an ancient ritual pilgrimage site

climb uphill to reach a crossroads, beside a large signboard, at **Shrone**. The route turns left here, but this is far enough for the day and a pick-up should be arranged in advance with a nearby accommodation provider.

There is no accommodation, shop or pub in Shrone. Rathmore is the nearest large village with a small range of services to offer, but it lies well off-route.

DAY 20
Shrone to Muckross

Start	Shrone (grid ref 134888)
Finish	Muckross (grid ref 978874)
Distance	20km (12.5 miles)
Cumulative Distance	514km (319.5 miles)
Maps	OSI Discovery 78 & 79
Terrain	Gently rolling country roads are used throughout
Refreshments	Spillane's Bar at Headford

There is no waymarked route between the Blackwater Way at Shrone and the Kerry Way at Muckross. In the previous edition of this guidebook, a road-walking route was suggested along the Clydagh Valley to Loo Bridge and Glenflesk, with the Lough Guitane Road finally leading to Muckross. However, since that time, a road-walking extension to the Blackwater Way has been suggested (though it hasn't yet been waymarked) via Headford, Brewsterfield and the Burmah Road. It includes fine views of the mountains and uses quiet country roads for the most part. Towards the end, the bustling tourist town of Killarney could be visited by making a short diversion off-route.

Leave the crossroads at **Shrone** by following a minor road in the direction of The Paps. Cross the **Beheenagh River**, then turn left at a junction, climbing uphill with views stretching from the mountains to the lowlands. The road rises and falls around **Gortacareen** and navigation is simply a matter of keeping left at road junctions. The Paps still dominate the countryside, while in the distance MacGillycuddy's Reeks form a jagged mountain profile. The road runs down to a river, passing a signpost for **Carraig an Aifrinn**, a 'Mass rock' where Catholics once gathered to pray during the times of the harsh penal laws.

THE IRISH COAST TO COAST WALK

Follow the road up through **Drom**, then downhill again to cross the **Owneyskeagh River**. The road climbs, passing under a railway bridge, to reach the R570 road at **Headford**. Turn left to pass a post office and Con Spillane's Bar.

The road passes under another railway bridge and passes a monument to one of the local 'flying columns' of the 1920s. Turn right along a minor road signposted for **Knockanes**, enjoying views from the higher parts, taking in Mangerton Mountain, Torc Mountain and MacGillycuddy's Reeks. Pass Knockanes National School and follow the undulating road until it drops to a junction with the busy N22 road at **Brewsterfield**. Turn right to walk alongside this road with care, then at the next junction turn left to leave it. ◄

The quiet road leaving the main road crosses a bridge over the **River Flesk**. Then you turn right up another minor road. This is a bendy, undulating road that passes houses and farms, and occasionally offers good views of nearby mountains, including: The Paps, Crohane, Bennaunmore, Stoompa, Mangerton Mountain,

If breaking the journey here, there are B&Bs along the main road to Killarney.

The two breast-like mountains known as The Paps dominate the scenery

Torc Mountain and MacGillycuddy's Reeks. Some parts of the road are wooded, and there are glimpses of the nearby river. Follow the road down to cross the **Finow River**, then walk up to a junction and turn right uphill, beside a forest with a margin of beech trees.

Pass **Loughquittane National School** and walk down the road, passing a series of B&B establishments (this is frustrating after days where they have been as scarce as hen's teeth!). Eventually the main N71 road is reached at **Muckross**, and a decision needs to be made. There are accommodation options in the area, and by turning left Muckross Post Office and Foodstore can be reached. A right turn, however, leads towards the big and bustling tourist resort of **Killarney**, which offers the fullest range of services seen for many a long day. Walkers who wish to continue walking can simply cross the road and follow a woodland path straight into the **Killarney National Park** to join the waymarked Kerry Way.

KILLARNEY

Killarney is of course one of Ireland's premier tourist destinations. The town is big and brash and offers every possible convenience. It is also off-route and not every walker would wish to make the detour. If anything is needed, however, then Killarney will no doubt be able to provide it, including outdoor gear if any of your kit has expired! Every type of accommodation is available, as well as banks with ATMs, a post office, an abundance of shops, toilets, and a bewildering variety of pubs and restaurants catering for every taste. There are regular Bus Éireann services, of which a few are summarised here: Table number 14 links Killarney with Limerick for services to Dublin. Table number 40 runs across country to Cork, Waterford and Rosslare Harbour. Table number 279 runs ahead to Glenbeigh and Cahersiveen, except Sunday, while table number 280 offers the complete Ring of Kerry scenic service in the summer months. Table number 286 links Killarney with the Kerry Airport for flights out of the area. The railway station offers services to Dublin, Cork and Limerick. To contact the tourist information office tel 064–31633.

STAGE 6
The Kerry Way

The rolling Atlantic Ocean beats the rugged cliff coast of Valentia Island (Day 24)

DAY 21
Muckross to Black Valley

Start	Muckross (grid ref 978874)
Finish	Black Valley Youth Hostel (grid ref 865828)
Distance	20km (12.5 miles)
Cumulative Distance	534km (332 miles)
Maps	OSI Discovery 78, OSI Killarney National Park
Terrain	Good low-level paths and tracks are used at first. Paths can be rugged at a higher level, as well as in woodlands later. In very wet weather the land near the Upper Lake can flood.
Refreshments	There are restaurants at Muckross House and Lord Brandon's Cottage, as well as snack provisions at Hillcrest in the Black Valley.

The Kerry Way is one of Ireland's premier waymarked trails. It starts by running through the Killarney National Park, leaving Muckross House and its gardens to discover Torc Waterfall. After climbing to the Old Kenmare Road, the route leads through The Wilderness where native Irish red deer thrive. The Kerry Way is very scenic and there are splendid views around the nearby mountains in clear weather. The route passes close to the Upper Lake on its way to the Black Valley. Bear in mind that accommodation in the valley is limited to a couple of B&Bs and a youth hostel, so it is wise to book a bed ahead, especially in the peak season.

Cross the main N71 road at **Muckross** and walk straight past a barrier to follow a grassy track into wonderful mature woodland. Cross a river and follow a narrower path through rhododendrons to reach the 15th-century Friary of Irrelagh, or **Muckross Friary**. Weave through the ruins and leave by following a clear path along an avenue of beech trees.

The Irish Coast to Coast Walk

KILLARNEY NATIONAL PARK

Senator Arthur Vincent presented the Muckross Estate to the Irish nation in 1932, stating that the area was to be managed 'as a national park for the general purpose of the recreation and enjoyment of the public'. Few people realise that Ireland therefore had a national park long before Britain. The Muckross Estate became known as the Bourn Vincent Memorial Park, but the land area was increased through land purchases in the 1970s, with the larger area being named the Killarney National Park.

Muckross House can be visited, and there is a National Park Visitor Centre round the back. There are gardens to explore, as well as a restaurant and toilets. Nearby farms display traditional farming methods and crafts, and rare Kerry cattle can be seen.

Turn right along a broad tarmac path, then walk straight ahead at a junction, signposted for Muckross House along a woodland path. Turn left as marked, and maybe take a spur path down to the shore of **Lough Leane** to see remarkable water-worn limestone islands and rocks, with mountains rising beyond. Continue along a lakeside path through mixed woodlands, then cross a broad tarmac path used by the Jarveys with their

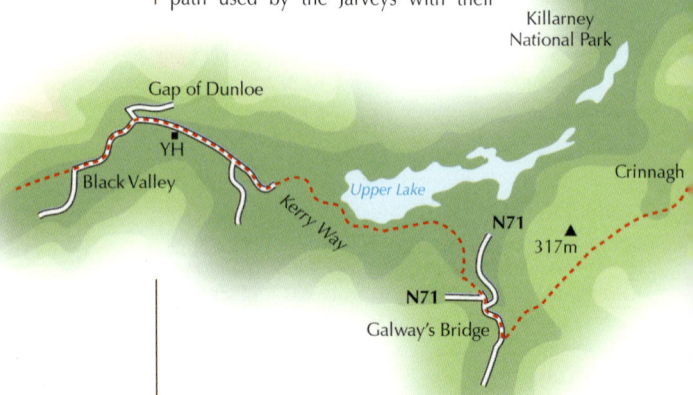

THE KERRY WAY: DAY 21 – MUCKROSS TO BLACK VALLEY

horse-drawn 'jaunting cars'. Walk along the path as marked, roughly parallel to the tarmac path, then later follow the tarmac path straight towards **Muckross House**.

As you approach **Muckross House**, turn right as signposted for Torc Waterfall. A broad tarmac path turns left, and the reedy **Muckross Lake** lies to the right. Follow the tarmac path at first, then veer left as signposted along a woodland path running parallel. There is another view of Muckross Lake from a clearing, then the route runs into woods again. Use an arched tunnel to avoid crossing the main road, then pass an information hut and follow a path to **Torc Waterfall**. The falls naturally look their best after heavy rain!

Enjoy the view of the falls from the bottom of the path. Once you climb up the steps and zig-zag higher up the rugged, wooded slopes, views are lost. Watch out for boulders and slippery tree roots on the ascent. Turn right at a path junction and cross a footbridge over the **Owengarriff River**. Turn left to continue upstream along a clear path. Continue straight along a track, which rises and climbs quite steeply at times, though never too far from the river.

155

THE IRISH COAST TO COAST WALK

Leave the woods to enter **The Wilderness**, which is the main red deer range in the national park. The open and rugged countryside is difficult to negotiate on foot, but the **Old Kenmare Road** is a clear track that is easy to follow. Follow the track uphill, noting a solitary ruined farmstead away to the left. The tussocky moorland alongside has patches of bracken and gorse, plus a few holly trees. Little spur paths at **Crinnagh** lead to splendid viewpoints at around 250m (820ft), which take in the nearby

Torc Waterfall, at the start of the Kerry Way, is a series of small cascades

THE KERRY WAY: DAY 21 – MUCKROSS TO BLACK VALLEY

lakes and mountains. The track later runs downhill and is flanked by tumbled, ruined enclosures. Continue along a narrow gravel path and cross a wobbly footbridge over the **Crinnagh River**.

The path weaves through a broad and boggy hollow dotted with odd trees and patchy woodlands. Walk upstream beside the river, crossing lengths of duckboard, then follow a rugged path up alongside contorted oak trees in **Esknamucky Glen**. There is a view back towards the bulky Mangerton Mountain as crude stone steps lead up the damp, narrow, rugged little glen. Continue along duckboards or rugged stone paths, always flanked by tussocky bogs. A longer duckboard path leads over a broad and boggy gap at 280m (920ft), and down to a building with a tin roof. Walk down a stony path into a mossy oakwood. Cross a footbridge over **Galway's River** and climb up a wooded slope. Walk downhill again to emerge from the woods and land on a track. Turn right and follow the track, which becomes a battered road, to a junction on the main N71 road between a bridge and **Derrycunnihy Church**.

Turn left along the road only to pass the church, then turn right to drop down from the road as signposted for the Kerry Way to the Black Valley. The path is rugged in places as it works through another mossy oakwood, with holly and rhododendron growing as an understorey. ▶

Walkers beside the Old Kenmare Road admire the MacGillycuddy's Reeks

There are duckboards in wet places, but also stony patches and tree roots ready to trip the unwary.

THE IRISH COAST TO COAST WALK

Rugged lowland scenery by the Upper Lake on the way to the Black Valley

Turn left at a signposted junction to follow a broader, easier path. This rises and falls, leaving the woods to enjoy views of the **Upper Lake** and surrounding mountains. The path is stony and crosses more tussocky bog. Pass **Lord Brandon's Cottage**, which has a restaurant and toilets. Go through a gate, cross a bridge over **Gearhameen River**, then go through another gate. Turn left as signposted for the Kerry Way, which is simply a matter of following a narrow road. Note a turning on the right for Hillcrest B&B, which offers snacks, but follow the road straight ahead, to continue into the **Black Valley**, passing the school to reach the Youth Hostel and church.

BLACK VALLEY

The rugged Black Valley lies in the shadow of Ireland's highest mountains: the mighty MacGillycuddy's Reeks. Facilities are limited to a couple of B&Bs and a youth hostel. Hillcrest B&B offers teas and snacks to passers-by, while the hostel has a small foodstore. This is a remote place to finish walking if your accommodation has not been secured, and the only transport out of the valley is an occasional afternoon boat service through the lakes to Ross Island near Killarney.

DAY 22
Black Valley to Glenbeigh

Start	Black Valley Youth Hostel (grid ref 865828)
Finish	Glenbeigh (grid ref 670911)
Distance	36km (22 miles)
Cumulative Distance	570km (354 miles)
Maps	OSI Discovery 78, OSI MacGillycuddy's Reeks
Terrain	Mostly along minor roads and farm tracks, but two rugged passes are crossed using mountain paths (care is needed on these paths). Forest paths and tracks are used later in the day, and another pass is crossed on a clear track.
Refreshments	The Climber's Inn at Glencar

This seems like a long day's walk through mountainous terrain, but apart from crossing three rugged passes, much of the route is along clear, low-level tracks and minor roads. There are impressive views of the mountains in clear weather. The route could be broken in Glencar, perhaps at the celebrated Climber's Inn, a long-time haunt of walkers and mountaineers. The Kerry Way crosses a very low shoulder of lofty Carrauntoohil, Ireland's highest mountain at 1039m (3414ft) in the rugged MacGillycuddy's Reeks. Anyone who feels drawn to make an ascent will certainly not finish in Glenbeigh the same day, and should make arrangements to stay in Glencar!

Leave the Black Valley Youth Hostel and walk along the road, further into the **Black Valley**. Keep left at a road junction, marked as a cul de sac, but signposted as the Kerry Way. Pass the **Shamrock Farmhouse** B&B and other houses, and keep straight on ahead at a road junction. Walk to a farm at the end of the road and turn left along a track. Go through a gate and go up a zig-zag near some small houses. A rugged track runs above a forest, crosses a rugged slope, then heads gently down along a rugged

The Irish Coast to Coast Walk

path through a broad forest ride. Leave the forest and cross a boulder-studded slope. Cross a small stile and go up a grassy track flanked by holly bushes. Pass a house at **Dromluska** and walk down its access track, then turn right up a narrow road with a grassy strip along its middle.

The road continues as a track towards the last farmhouse in the valley, with the steep and rocky slopes of **Broaghnabinnia** rising on the left. Go through a gate to approach the farm, but keep to the right to pass around the back of it as marked. Continue straight up the boulder-strewn, boggy glen-head, aiming for the lowest gap in view ahead. Marker posts show the best way forward, but keep well to the right of a **standing stone** on the gap, to cross a small stile over a fence at around 300m (985ft). Watch carefully for marker posts and yellow arrows painted on rocks to forge a way down a rugged nose at **Bridia**, avoiding the little valleys on either

THE KERRY WAY: DAY 22 – BLACK VALLEY TO GLENBEIGH

side. Watch carefully towards the bottom as the path shifts to the right.

Turn left to follow a vague track alongside a fence round the head of the valley, which leads to a small farm. Follow the vague access track away from the farm, crossing the valley to reach a minor road. Turn left through a gate and follow the road down through the valley. Another farm is reached in a patch of mixed woodland at **Maghanlawaun**, where a Kerry Way signpost points to a small stile next to old gate piers. Walk up a small field and cross another small stile over a fence. Follow the zig-zag route as marked, up the **Lack Road** ▶ Enjoy widening views across the valley, then cross another small stile over a fence. The zig-zag path climbs at a reasonable gradient, despite the steep and rugged slope, however, it becomes narrower and more rugged on upper slopes of gorse scrub. Looking back, Broaghnabinnia dominates the mountain scene more than the much loftier MacGillycuddy's Reeks.

Cross a stile over a fence on top of the gap and climb a little further to around 370m (1215ft) before descending. The path crosses steep, rocky, heathery and boggy ground that needs care. When the **Gearhanagour Stream** is reached, turn left to head downstream. The path becomes a rugged track,

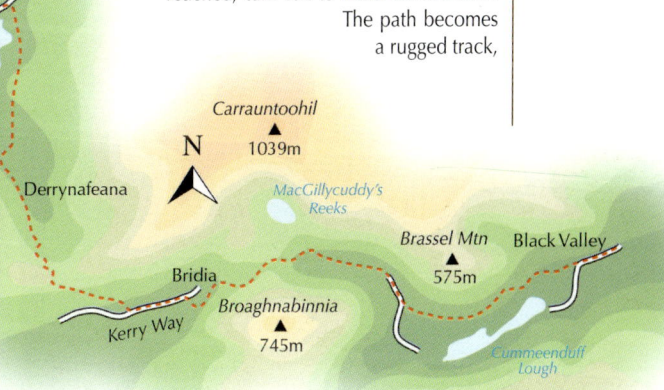

Lack Road is an old mountain track running up boulder-studded grassy slopes.

THE IRISH COAST TO COAST WALK

The view from the Kerry Way on the Lack Road in the rugged Bridia Valley

The Kerry Way: Day 22 – Black Valley to Glenbeigh

Walking on the lower part of the Lack Road on the way to Lough Acoose

which eventually turns round a corner to pass a farm and some ruins at **Derrynafeana**. Follow the track across the river, rising through forest and continuing along a narrow road. Pass easily through a rugged gap and continue alongside **Lough Acoose** to reach a road junction. The Lough Acoose House B&B is here at **Coornameena**, if a break is needed at this point. Turn left along the road, still beside Lough Acoose, to continue. The road passes an old IRA memorial and runs down through a forested glen to reach a signposted junction. Accommodation options are signposted to the right, but the Kerry Way keeps left to leave the forest and arrive at the **Climber's Inn**. B&B and hostel accommodation is available here, as well as a campsite and food and drink. There is also a post office and shop in the building.

If not stopping at the Climber's Inn, turn left along a track and pass a couple of houses, and some woodland and bog, before reaching a road. Keep right as signposted for the Kerry Way to reach a junction. Turn left to cross the **River Caragh**, which drains a broad, boggy landscape surrounded by mountains. Turn right downstream as sign-

THE IRISH COAST TO COAST WALK

posted for the Kerry Way. The river is confined to a deep, long, rock-walled pool for some length. Above the river, ridges of rock separated by boggy patches act as speed bumps to slow the hurrying walker, but a level, grassy riverside path comes later.

Turn left away from the river, into a forest. Turn right along a grassy ride flanked by birch trees. A more gravelly track continues through a partially-felled area where substantial numbers of birch trees remain standing. There is quite a mixture of tree species as the track runs along and up to a barrier. Turn right gently down a road, then left up past a barrier onto another forest track. The track gives way to a path with crude stone steps leading up to a lowly viewpoint at **Lickeen**. Enjoy views of the mountains and Lough Caragh. The path wriggles about, up and down steps in the forest, then a grassy track leads down to a barrier and a road.

The Kerry Way crosses the Windy Gap between Glencar and Glenbeigh

THE KERRY WAY: DAY 22 – BLACK VALLEY TO GLENBEIGH

Turn left up the road, which rises and falls, passing woods and small fields, crossing the **Meelagh River** and Owbeg River. Climb almost to a **school**, but veer left along a narrow road signposted as the Kerry Way. The road climbs alongside a forest and swings left. The tarmac expires and a clear track bends sharply to the right as it climbs. Take a sharp left turn at **Gortdirragh** and follow a clear, grassy track through a gate. This becomes stonier as it climbs, and there is another gate near the top. Look back from the **Windy Gap**, around 340m (1115ft), towards MacGillycuddy's Reeks and other mountains beyond the broad, boggy, wooded valley.

Follow a stony hollow way downhill. There are views of the large village of Glenbeigh and the steep hill behind it, as well as part of Dingle Bay, which suggests that the end of the Coast to Coast Walk could be close! The mountains of the Dingle Peninsula rise beyond the bay. The path drifts to the right and becomes an access road serving a few houses at **Gowlane**. The road later turns left and runs down to another road (where there is a picnic table). Turn right along and down the road to land in the middle of **Glenbeigh**.

GLENBEIGH

This lively little tourist village has plenty of facilities, including a range of accommodation, a post office and a few shops, pubs and restaurants. Bus Éireann table number 279 offers daily links (except on Sunday) ahead to Caherciveen and back to Killarney. Table number 280 is a daily summertime tour around the celebrated scenic Ring of Kerry.

DAY 23
Glenbeigh to Cahersiveen

Start	Glenbeigh (grid ref 670991)
Finish	Cahersiveen (grid ref 472795)
Distance	28km (17.5 miles)
Cumulative Distance	598km (371.5 miles)
Maps	OSI Discovery 70, 78 & 83
Terrain	Forest tracks and roads give way to rugged mountain tracks and bog roads, with some road-walking and occasional linking paths.
Refreshments	None on the route

If time is pressing, the Irish Coast to Coast Walk could be brought to a speedy conclusion by finishing on the shores of Dingle Bay down the road from Glenbeigh. Walkers who are in no great hurry will appreciate that they are in a wonderful part of the world and will be happy to continue towards Cahersiveen and Valentia Island. The Kerry Way is waymarked all the way to Cahersiveen along a series of old highways and bog roads. The current main road, used by all the Ring of Kerry traffic, bears no relation to the old coach road that was carved around the mountainsides and is now used by the Kerry Way, or the railway line that followed in later years (which has since been closed). Walkers intending to make use of the seasonal ferry to Valentia Island are reminded that its running times should be checked in advance.

Follow the main N71 road down through **Glenbeigh** and turn right, as signposted for the Kerry Way, along the beach road. Cross the **River Behy** using a six-arched stone bridge, then turn right. Branch left at a parking space and picnic site to follow a clear path up into a forest. Turn sharp left uphill as marked. The path more or less levels out and contours round the steep, forested hillside – there is quite a mix of tree species. Then at a junction, branch right and later descend to a road. Turn

THE KERRY WAY: DAY 23 – GLENBEIGH TO CAHERSIVEEN

MOUNTAIN STAGE

The name refers to the time when horse-drawn coaches were hauled round the mountainside between Glenbeigh and Cahersiveen. It was customary for horse teams to be changed at stages along the way. Hence, the Mountain Stage was where the team climbing from Glenbeigh would be changed for another team, who would take travellers on and around the mountainside.

right up the road and climb gradually, with increasingly fine views of surrounding mountains. Go straight through a crossroads at **Drom**, as signposted for the Kerry Way. The road runs along, then down to cross a dip, with a view of Dingle Bay and the mountainous Dingle Peninsula off to the right. Walk uphill and turn left as signposted, crossing the main N71 road using a bridge. The main road sits on the course of an old railway line here at **Mountain Stage**.

Turn right as signposted for the Kerry Way and walk down a quiet road parallel to the main road, again with a view of Dingle Bay and the mountains. Watch for a grassy track marked on the left, rising among a few trees. This quickly becomes a rough and stony track leading through a gate. The track climbs more easily and reaches a huddle of **ruined buildings**, where there is another gate. A more rugged stretch rises across the hillside, passing through several gates, with increasingly wide-ranging views of the mountains. ▶

The mountain track, once a highway in its heyday, runs easily across a very steep slope and onwards up a heathery slope. Cross a little gap on a shoulder of **Drung Hill** above Gleensk around 330m (1080ft). Walk down gentle, boggy slopes with a view down to the old railway viaduct at Gleensk. ▶ Cross a stream and follow a grassier track gently downhill through the forest at **Coomshanna**, then rise gently to a gate and ladder stile to leave the forest. The track runs alongside a fence above a series of turf cuttings, and there is a gate along the way. Pass some **ruined cottages** and go through more gates while following the track downhill to a gate and a minor road.

Note the curious sandspits that poke out into the waters of Dingle Bay, and look back along the route for a glimpse of MacGillycuddy's Reeks. The view down the mountainside reveals a series of embankments, cuttings and tunnels along the line of the old railway which run parallel to the main road.

The mountain of Knocknadobar dominates the view ahead, while other hills crowd around Cahersiveen in the distance. Valentia Island is in view, but is difficult to distinguish as an island.

167

THE IRISH COAST TO COAST WALK

The Kerry Way uses a rugged old track in the shadow of Knocknadobar

Turn left along the road, then right at a gate and stile. A boggy hollow way leads to another gate and stile, after which the route continues very wet and boggy as it runs alongside a fence. Look ahead to spot other gates, stiles and markers, and walk alongside another fence before the route descends gently with fences on both sides at **Meelin**. There are some trees on the left, while the track runs straight ahead as a firm, grassy way between embankments and bushes. A road is reached at a house at **Boulerdah**. Keep right, then left at a road junction to continue straight ahead and downhill. Walk straight past another road junction and pass a forest to reach another junction at **Foilmore**. Turn left along an old 'Mass path', through little kissing gates and down a brambly path to reach a rickety footbridge. Follow markers off to the right, crossing another footbridge to reach a road at **Gortmore**.

Turn right and pass a Gaelic Football ground, then turn left up a track. Walk to the top of the track (avoiding turnings to a couple of houses). Swing right and cross a stile by a gate to land in a mudbath. Walk alongside an old hollow way, crossing stiles beside gates to reach a farm road. Turn left up towards an art studio at **Teeraha**, then turn right along and up a clear track. The Kerry Way is signposted uphill from a gate and ladder stile, but stay on the track and walk straight ahead to take a waymarked spur route to distant Cahersiveen. A battered road with a grassy strip along its middle is followed, and you keep to the right and eventually cross a cattle grid. Turn left to reach a road junction at **Srugreana**.

THE IRISH COAST TO COAST WALK

A walker on an old, straight bog road from Inchimacteige to Cahersiveen

Turn left, then almost immediately right to walk down a track. This passes fields and later has a small stream alongside. Turn left along a road, then right to cross a footbridge over the **Carhan River**. Follow a clear bog road at **Inchimacteige** and continue straight onwards to **Chiclog**. Turn right at a road junction and walk down to **Carhan Bridge**, keeping right at road junctions, or popping into the **Daniel O'Connell Memorial Park** that has been established between the old and new road bridges. Turn left along the main N71 road and walk straight into **Cahersiveen** to avail yourself of all its facilities.

THE KERRY WAY: DAY 23 – GLENBEIGH TO CAHERSIVEEN

CAHERSIVEEN

A bust of Daniel O'Connell on the outskirts of Cahersiveen

The ruined building at Carhan Bridge was the birthplace of Daniel O'Connell, otherwise known as The Liberator, who was born in 1775. It was near his monument back in Dublin that you began the Irish Coast to Coast Walk. Standing here within sight of the Atlantic Ocean, the big, bustling city of Dublin seems a whole world away! The Catholic church in the middle of town is known as the Daniel O'Connell Memorial Church. One of O'Connell's greatest triumphs was Catholic Emancipation.

Cahersiveen has everything the weary walker needs, and the Old Barracks Visitor Centre contains plenty of historical artefacts and notes about the heritage of the town. The Barracks were burnt in the Troubles of the 1920s, but have been completely restored and have a Disneyesque appearance down by the Valentia River.

There is plenty of accommodation, including an independent hostel, banks with ATMs, a post office, plenty of shops, toilets, and several pubs and restaurants. Almost everything is lined up alongside a main street of colour, clutter and character. Bus Éireann table number 279 offers daily links (except on Sundays) back to Glenbeigh and Killarney. Table number 280 is a daily summertime tour around the celebrated scenic Ring of Kerry.

At this point you should think ahead and phone the Valentia Island ferry for the following morning to ensure that they are running (tel 066–9476377). It might also be a good idea to take the phone numbers of a couple of local taxi drivers, just in case you need to be collected at the end of the last day's walk, where there are no bus services available. There is a tourist information office in the centre of Cahersiveen (tel 066–9472589).

THE IRISH COAST TO COAST WALK

DAY 24
Cahersiveen to Portmagee

Start	Cahersiveen (grid ref 472795)
Finish	Portmagee (grid ref 373730)
Distance	25km (15.5 miles)
Cumulative Distance	623km (387 miles)
Maps	OSI Discovery 83
Terrain	Mostly easy road-walking, followed by a short but rugged cliff walk
Refreshments	There is a pub at Reenard Point, pubs, restaurants and shops at Knightstown and pubs, restaurants and shop at Portmagee.

All things must come to an end, and the Irish Coast to Coast Walk finally runs out of land where the south-west coast drops abruptly into the Atlantic Ocean. The last part of the route is not waymarked, but simply follows roads from Cahersiveen to Reenard Point, where a seasonal ferry leads across to Valentia Island. Quiet roads lead along the length of the island, then a rugged cliff coast walk makes a circuit around Bray Head. This is a fitting place to end as you look out across the broad Atlantic Ocean, but in practical terms you will have to walk across a bridge to finish in the village of Portmagee. Portmagee is probably the safest place to dip your feet in the sea and conclude the walk. All that remains is to plan your departure from there.

Follow the main N71 road out of **Cahersiveen**. It is called Valentia Road and it passes the **Met Éireann Valentia Observatory**. If you have been keeping a note of local weather forecasts recently, this is where they originate. Turn right down a road signposted for Reenard Point, passing a few B&Bs along the way, and enjoying glimpses of a rather attractive coastline to the right. The remote Blasket Islands nudge into view at one point – they are the most westerly part of Europe! A fish-packing plant is

THE KERRY WAY: DAY 24 – CAHERSIVEEN TO PORTMAGEE

reached near the end of the point – there is a handy seafood bar opposite if you have to shelter while waiting for a ferry on **Reenard Point**. The seasonal car ferry should be checked in advance (tel 066–9476377), or your walk could grind to a halt at this point! The ferry trip is over in mere minutes. Step ashore at **Knightstown** on Valentia Island.

KNIGHTSTOWN

The little harbour at Knightstown features a distinctive clock, backed by the Royal Pier Bar. The village can be explored fairly quickly, though most of its points of interest can be seen while following the route. The Valentia Heritage Centre explains the history of the Transatlantic Cable, linking Europe and America, which fed into the ocean via Valentia Island. Glanleam House and its subtropical gardens can be visited by detouring from the route later.

Facilities include a small range of accommodation options, including a youth hostel and an independent hostel, a post office, shop, toilets, and a few pubs and restaurants. There are no bus services, though there are taxis available.

Walk through the village along the R565 road, but turn right at St John the Baptist Church of Ireland as signposted for the museum. The **Valentia Heritage Centre** is on the right later, along with the old lighthouse keeper's cottages. Views to the right take in the mountainous Dingle Peninsula and Blasket Islands. Keep straight ahead at a road junction, though bear in mind that you could detour right to visit Glanleam House and its subtropical gardens. Pass an old church tower and keep right at a junction where a left turn is signposted for **Kylemore Burial Ground**. The road runs across a steep slope of mixed woodland, with an understorey of rhododendron and fuschia, and a lush ground cover of St Patrick's Cabbage. When a staggered crossroads is reached, turn sharp left uphill, then take the next turn up to the right. The road runs level and there is a view along the length of the Portmagee Channel to the left. ▶

Eventually, after passing farms and houses at **Feaghmaan**, go straight through a crossroads. Look to the

> Portmagee and its bridge can be seen, along with the distinctive signal tower on Bray Head, and the pyramidal Skelligs far out to sea.

THE IRISH COAST TO COAST WALK

A standing stone passed near a crossroads in the middle of Valentia Island

left to spot a **standing stone**, but otherwise keep following the road, which runs gradually downhill. Walk uphill and note a few deer pens off to the right, then reach a road junction at **Coarha Beg**. Turn right as signposted for St Brendan's Well and follow a clear track downhill and across a broad bog. The bog road turns

The Kerry Way: Day 24 – Cahersiveen to Portmagee

left and right, passing three isolated houses, then a boggy path leads alongside an embankment to **St Brendan's Well**. There is a well, an altar and a few crude, ancient slate slab crosses with a ladder stile between them.

Take a short-cut back onto the bog-road and follow it a short way until it expires. Follow a straggly line of large stones across the bog, with a path alongside, to reach an area of short grass and thrift on top of rugged cliffs near **Beennakryaka Head**. Turn left to follow the cliff line, avoiding narrow chasms along the way. Later, stay seawards of fencing and climb gradually uphill on **Beenanillar Head**, enjoying remarkable cliff views. Step inland of the fence on a steep, rocky, heathery climb, reaching a moorland crest of short grass and heather at 239m (784ft). Enjoy views of the Blasket Islands, countless mountain peaks along the Dingle Peninsula and through the Iveragh Peninsula, taking in headlands far beyond Valentia Island, as well as the rocky peaks of Great and Little Skellig out to sea. Walk down to the old Marconi Signal Tower on **Bray Head** and pause to register the fact that the Irish Coast to Coast Walk is essentially over. ▶

In practical terms, however, the finish must be elsewhere. Turn around and follow the access track downhill from the tower. Go past a gate and ladder stile and continue to a small parking space at **Clynacartan**. Follow

Take a while to think back along the journey from one side of Ireland to the other, and think about the variety of scenery, history and heritage you experienced along the way.

THE IRISH COAST TO COAST WALK

The precipitous cliffs of Bray Head mark the end of the Coast to Coast Walk

THE KERRY WAY: DAY 24 – CAHERSIVEEN TO PORTMAGEE

the road onwards to a junction at the **Telegraph Field**.

There is a monument to the Transatlantic Telegraph Cable situated here. This was where the first message was sent from Valentia to America in 1858; from Queen Victoria to President Buchanan. A timeline shows that the first cable, laid in 1857, was a failure, and a succession of eight cables were laid up until 1894, the last of which served all the way through to 1965.

Follow the road to the right, and it later bends left and reaches a junction. Turn right to pass the **Skellig Heritage Centre** and cross the bridge to reach the village of **Portmagee** back on the mainland.

PORTMAGEE

The mouth of Portmagee Channel seen on the way to Portmagee

This fine village is a practical place to end the Irish Coast to Coast Walk. The Skellig Heritage Centre focusses on the last battered pieces of Ireland, where for centuries hermit monks braved all kinds of weather out on the Skelligs. There are boat trips available if anyone wishes to extend their explorations further offshore!

Facilities include a couple of B&Bs in the village and surrounding countryside, a post office shop, toilets and a couple of pubs and restaurants. There are no bus services, so plan ahead to ensure a smooth departure, maybe calling on the services of a local taxi to return to Cahersiveen.

LEAVING THE IRISH COAST TO COAST WALK

There are no bus services from Valentia Island or Portmagee. The nearest bus service is from Cahersiveen. Bus Éireann table number 279 currently runs at 08h05 each morning (except Sunday) from Cahersiveen to Killarney. It links with table number 14 to Limerick, where table number 12 continues to Dublin, reaching the city by 16h10 the same day. Alternatively, switch to trains at Killarney to reach Dublin by 13h55 the same day.

Bus Éireann table number 40 offers occasional cross-country runs from Killarney to Rosslare Harbour for ferries to Wales. Bus Éireann table number 14 leaves Killarney and stops on request at Kerry Airport, allowing for a speedy exit using flights to Dublin or London. From Limerick, Bus Éireann table number 343 runs regularly to Shannon Airport. With carefully thought-out bus, rail and air connections, you could leave Cahersiveen in the morning and be home the same evening!

Valentia Island is separated from the mainland by Portmagee Channel

HIGH-LEVEL ALTERNATIVE ROUTES

The waymarked trails making up the Irish Coast to Coast Walk are generally routed through fairly low-lying countryside. The Wicklow Way climbs above 500–600m (1640–1970ft) in places, but most other trails rarely rise to that height and for the most part stay well below 300m (985ft). Long-distance walkers sometimes find themselves following minor roads or forest tracks along the foot of mountain ranges, and may wonder if there are any routes that would take them through the wilder upland landscapes. There are many places where walkers can enjoy high-level alternative routes, but remember that these are not waymarked, so you have to do your own route-finding. While access to the uplands may be tolerated by landowners, there is often no legal right-of-way, so you must be on your best behaviour. Also, bear in mind that these routes can be difficult to negotiate safely in foul weather, so ensure that your experience is equal to the task.

Seven alternative high-level routes are offered here for competent hill-walkers and careful navigators, but the route descriptions are given only in outline form. You have to locate good access routes to the mountains when you leave the waymarked trails, and use map and compass to find your own way from summit to summit. Take care not to damage walls and fences, and use gates and stiles wherever these are provided.

The Lug Walk through the Wicklow Mountains or the rugged trek along the crest of MacGillycuddy's Reeks are established classics. High-level routes along the Blackstairs, Comeragh and Knockmealdown Mountains, or the circuit of the Coomasaharn Horseshoe, are becoming more popular. The rugged traverse of the Derrynasaggart Mountains is seldom attempted as a day walk, though The Paps do attract a number of walkers in their own right.

All the high-level routes are described so that you can see where they break off from the waymarked trails, and link back into them later. The daily Coast to Coast Walk schedules may need to be altered significantly if these upland options are taken, and the choice of accommodation might become very limited. Bear this in mind for when you are descending from the mountains tired and hungry at the end of a long day!

The Lug Walk is very long and difficult and is unlikely to be completed within a day, but most of the other alternatives make fine one-day walks.

The Irish Coast to Coast Walk

The Lug Walk *(Days 3, 4, 5)*

Start	Knockree Youth Hostel
Finish	Aughavannagh
Distance	66km (41 miles)
Maps	OSI Discovery 56 & 62, Harvey Maps' *Wicklow Mountains*

The Lug Walk is a Wicklow Mountains classic, but any attempt to cover the distance should be based on a rigorous assessment of your stamina and ability, to say nothing of the weather and the number of daylight hours available to you. The Lug Walk can replace Day 3, Day 4 and part of *Day 5* of the Irish Coast to Coast Walk, and runs from Knockree Youth Hostel to Aughavannagh, linking back into the Wicklow Way at the Iron Bridge. If a break is needed along the way, the only practicable point at which to leave the route is on the Wicklow Gap, where the R756 road crosses the route. The full distance covered on this alternative is 66km (41 miles), compared to the Wicklow Way between the same points, which measures 56km (35 miles).

Be warned that the Lug Walk crosses the most bleak, boggy and desolate parts of the Wicklow Mountains, where progress is hampered by decaying blanket bogs cut into awkward hags and groughs. Foul weather makes it much worse. The altitude ranges from 400–925m and there are no habitations or facilities along the way. The only roads crossed are the Sally Gap and the Wicklow Gap, which are two of the highest motor roads in Ireland.

Leave **Knockree Youth Hostel** and follow the road up through **Glencree** to reach a former barracks building. Follow the road further uphill then start climbing the rugged slopes above it. At the top of the slope, keeping well away from the cliffs fringing **Lower Lough Bray**, a tall TV mast can be seen on Kippure in clear weather. Aim towards it, crossing difficult ground that steepens before

HIGH-LEVEL ALTERNATIVE ROUTES – THE LUG WALK

the mast is reached. The 757m (2475ft) summit of **Kippure** is the highest point in Co Dublin, though the other side of the rather worn-looking mountain top is in Co Wicklow.

No-one would blame walkers for following the access road downhill from the TV mast, which saves a difficult slog across the southern slopes of Kippure. The access road links with the R115 road at a clump of bushes. This is also known as the **Military Road**; follow it across Liffey Head Bridge to reach a crossroads at **Sally Gap**. Climb up the steep slope south-west of the gap, which is covered in deep heather. A clear path traces the course of an old boundary ditch uphill. The stony trough of the ditch offers a fairly firm footing and leads to the 682m (2244ft) summit of **Carrigvore**, where a few boulders are scattered across the moorland.

Boggy patches are crossed as the boundary ditch descends from Carrigvore. After crossing a gap, there is a two-stage ascent of **Gravale**, which is separated by a level area of bog. The 718m (2352ft) summit has a cairn, though there are also some large boulders around. After leaving the summit, descend past more boulders and continue down a rugged slope to land on a broad and

A view along the broad and boggy moorland crest to Mullaghcleevaun

181

THE IRISH COAST TO COAST WALK

boggy gap. A steep slope rises beyond the gap, and the ground is rather wrinkled and proves difficult underfoot. However, the 720m (2364ft) summit of **Duff Hill** is easier to cross and it bears a cairn and a few boulders. Views in all directions appear quite desolate.

There is an easy descent from Duff Hill and this high-level route keeps to the crest of the range to cross another broad gap. The next ascent is fairly gentle, and as the blanket bog has washed away in places, simply walk up a stony slope that offers a firm, dry surface. A minor rise is crossed while following the broad moorland crest, on the way to **Mullaghcleevaun East Top** at 795m (2615ft). There are large granite blocks here, as well as a cairn. A descent westwards leads across a broad area of black peat, then a broad shoulder leads up to the summit of **Mullaghcleevaun**, where a trig point stands at 849m (2788ft). The short grass is studded by a number of large boulders, one of which has a memorial fixed to it. There are splendid views all around the Wicklow wilderness.

Heading south from Mullaghcleevaun, note that the moorland crest swings south-east before an approach is made to the little hump of **Barnacullian** at 714m (2342ft). The ground is a mess of peat hags and groughs in places, and the view ahead would lead some walkers to despair. However, there is a feature known as the **Green Road** that can be used, where the blanket bog ends abruptly just before the eastern slopes become too steep to traverse. More rapid progress can be made towards Tonelagee, which is climbed in two stages. First the 714m (2342ft) summit of **Stoney Top** is gained, then a slight descent leads across a stony gap. Another steep pull leads up to the 817m (2686ft) summit of **Tonelagee**, where there is a trig point and cairn. Looking ahead to distant Lugnaquillia is enough to make most walkers consider taking a break, so descend roughly south-west to reach the R756 road on the **Wicklow Gap**. Arrange to be collected at this point, or face a long walk down through Glendasan to find accommodation around Glendalough for the night. ◀

Walkers can of course join the course of the Wicklow Way again in Glendalough, but if they are game for more thrashing about in the bleak heart of the Wicklow wilderness, then they can return to the Wicklow Gap.

HIGH-LEVEL ALTERNATIVE ROUTES – THE LUG WALK

Follow a twisting tarmac road from the gap to the top of **Turlough Hill**, where there is a reservoir and a concrete tower. Purist walkers can step to one side and aim instead for a nearby summit at 681m (2228ft) that has a more natural appearance.

TURLOUGH HILL

This is a strange place, dominated not by a shapely peak and cairn, but by a reservoir and a concrete tower – all part of a hydro-electric Pumped Storage Scheme. Despite being a blight on the wilderness, this feat of engineering is popular with visitors and there are sometimes minibus rides up to the reservoir.

In mist the next stretch can be particularly tricky as there is no path, plenty of bog, and the only aid to navigation is the appearance of little **Lough Firrib**. From the lough, either head south-west to gain the 734m (2421ft) summit of **Conavalla**, or simply omit the summit and pass the Three Lakes on the way to the 701m (2302ft) summit of **Table Mountain**. This is an area of near-level black peat, but there is a small cairn in the middle of it all. Head roughly southwards and cross the course of the **Table Track** near a prominent notice erected by the Army.

The route progresses round the boundary of the Glen of Imaal Artillery Range. There is no danger on the perimeter, but take care not to stray westwards into the range. A few waymark posts have been planted over **Camenabologue**, and as most of the blanket bog has gone from the hill, the ascent is on a firm surface. The 758m (2495ft) summit is easily reached and bears a large cairn. Descend slightly east of south to cross a broad, hummocky gap. Once across the gap, an ascent in stages leads over a little bump on **Cannow Mountain** at 712m (2336ft), then a broader crest finally snakes towards the summit of **Lugnaquillia**. There is a useful path along the way, and the summit area is flat and grassy, with a trig point at 925m (3039ft) alongside a large platform cairn. ▶

To descend towards Aughavannagh and keep away from forests, use the following route: walk a short way

A view indicator helps walkers to make the most of the views, while a walk around the summit reveals the cliffs of the North and South Prisons. Lugnaquillia is the highest mountain in Co Wicklow and the Province of Leinster.

THE IRISH COAST TO COAST WALK

Snow and ice crusts the platform cairn on the summit of Lugnaquillia

west of the summit cairn on Lugnaquillia, then descend steeply south-west to reach a level gap of black peat. Beyond this, a short ascent leads to the 759m (2501ft) summit of **Slievemaan**. Leave the summit cairn and descend south-east, before swinging southwards along a heathery crest to reach the little hump of **Lybagh**. Continue descending south-eastwards to reach the edge of a forest, then follow the forest fence for a while. Move away from the forest and follow a track down towards a solitary farm in the Ow Valley. The farm access road leads to a minor road at **Aughavannagh**, and roads can be followed to the **Iron Bridge** to link back into the course of the Wicklow Way. Follow the waymarked trail for a couple of days and build up your strength for the next high-level alternative!

Blackstairs Mountains *(Days 7 and 8)*

Start	Kildavin
Finish	Graiguenamanagh
Distance	50km (31 miles)
Map	OSI Discovery 68

A walk along the length of the Blackstairs Mountains offers walkers a high-level alternative to the South Leinster Way between Kildavin and Graiguenamanagh, replacing *Day 7* and part of *Day 8* of the Coast to Coast Walk. Most of that part of the South Leinster Way is either low-level, or runs largely along roads. This high-level route follows the South Leinster Way out of Kildavin, but keeps climbing to reach the summit of Mount Leinster, then runs across the Scullogue Gap to continue along the crest of the Blackstairs Mountains. After descending from the mountains near Glynn, walkers might as well head down to the tidal limit of the River Barrow at St Mullins, and follow the towpath to Graiguenamanagh. The high-level distance from Kildavin to Graiguenamanagh is 50km (31 miles). Bear in mind that the South Leinster Way between those two places is only 34km (21 miles).

Leave **Kildavin** in the company of the South Leinster Way, following a farm access road and forest tracks to climb between Greenoge Hill and **Kilbrannish Hill**. The South Leinster Way follows a road up towards the **Corrabut Gap**, then follows a road signposted for the Nine Stones. After passing through a forest on this road, leave the road and climb straight up the steep and heathery slopes of Mount Leinster. The going is quite difficult up the **Black Banks**, but this is a more natural line than using the access road serving the TV mast. The slope levels out for a while before a final pull leads up to the 792m (2610ft) summit of **Mount Leinster**. ▶

The boundary between Co Carlow and Co Wexford is followed practically all the way along the length of the Blackstairs Mountains to complete this high-level

There is a trig point and a cairn, and despite the mast, there are wide-ranging views on a clear day. The summit is the highest point in Co Carlow and Co Wexford. This is the highest point in Ireland that can be reached by ordinary vehicles, so expect to find company on fine weekends!

185

THE IRISH COAST TO COAST WALK

traverse. Descend from Mount Leinster in a southerly direction, picking a way down a steep and rugged slope. A series of old bog roads are now largely overgrown, but they lead further downhill and across the slopes of **Knockroe**. Allow yourself to be funnelled onto a stony track, which continues as a farm access road down to the **Scullogue Gap**. There are actually two roads crossing the gap, so cross both of them to reach a small forest.

Use a forest track and forest ride to reach the open slopes of the Blackstairs Mountains. A steep climb leads uphill, then the gradient eases and the slope is littered with countless boulders. The top of **Blackstairs Mountain** is an area of peat hags bearing a cairn at 735m (2409ft). Head roughly south-westwards to descend, passing huge blocks of rock known as **Caher Roe's Den** (Caher Roe was a robber of some repute). An old track is crossed on a gap, then a climb leads along the next stretch of the ridge.

Forests have been planted all along the eastern flank of the Blackstairs Mountains, but by following the forest fence along the crest of the ridge, you will generally have an open slope running down towards the

Mount Leinster is the highest point in both Co Carlow and Co Wexford

HIGH-LEVEL ALTERNATIVE ROUTES – BLACKSTAIRS MOUNTAINS

broad vale drained by the River Barrow. **Carrigalackan** is the first summit on this part of the ridge, at 463m (1523ft). It is followed by **Carrigroe** at 495m (1628ft) and **Dho Bran** at 504m (1679ft). Follow the ridge onwards and start to descend more steeply, but keep heading south-westwards towards the spur of **Dranagh Mountain**. There is a forest here, with a clear track that leads quickly and easily down from the hills. The track runs into a network of minor roads before reaching the R729 road. This can be followed to **Glynn**, from where a short walk leads down to the old monastic village of **St Mullins**, where there is a little accommodation. Continue down to the tidal reaches of the **River Barrow**. A fine towpath leads upstream alongside the river to link with the South Leinster Way again at the bustling little town of **Graiguenamanagh**.

An iron cross perched on a rocky edge in the Blackstairs Mountains

The Irish Coast to Coast Walk

Comeragh Mountains *(Days 11 and 12)*

Start	Harney's Cross Roads
Finish	Fourmilewater
Distance	36km (22 miles)
Map	OSI Discovery 75

The East Munster Way merely toys with the foothills of the Comeragh Mountains, but this upland alternative strikes through the very heart of the range. It can replace half of *Day 11* and most of *Day 12* of the waymarked Coast to Coast Walk. The shapely ridge of Knockanaffrin, which is seen on the forest walk above Kilsheelan, is traversed along its entire length. A prominent gap, known simply as The Gap, is crossed. A steep climb leads onto the desperately boggy central plateau of the Comeragh Mountains. After thrashing around and squelching along this broad crest, a gradual descent leads into the Nire Valley, where a road-walk leads through Ballymacarbry to link with the course of the East Munster Way again at Fourmilewater. The distance taken by this high-level route between the East Munster Way at Harney's Cross Roads and the return to the waymarked trail at Fourmilewater is 36km (22 miles). The East Munster Way between those two points measures 21km (13 miles) and is of course much easier.

There is an independent hostel at Powers the Pot near Harney's Cross Roads, and there are a couple of B&Bs in the Nire Valley towards the end of the walk. Bear in mind that the boggy parts of the Comeragh Mountains are really very boggy and this high-level route should be avoided after periods of heavy rain.

Head south-east from **Harney's Cross Roads**, following a minor road for a short way and crossing a bridge over a river. There is access to open ground leading towards the Knockanaffrin ridge. Be warned that this is a rugged tract of country featuring deep heather, boggy patches and hidden holes full of water. However, by plodding onwards towards the mountain, progress becomes easier as height is gained. First, there is a steep and rugged

HIGH-LEVEL ALTERNATIVE ROUTES – COMERAGH MOUNTAINS

View from Sgilloge Lough to Knockanaffrin in the Comeragh Mountains

climb onto **Shauneenabreaga** at 530m (1740ft). This is a small summit on the end of a spur and there are other similar features along the ridge. Beyond this line of false tops is the 678m (2181ft) summit of **Knocksheegowna**. This is easily identified because there is a trig point lurking to one side of a rocky peak.

Continue along the rocky ridge, descending a little to cross a grassy, bouldery gap overlooking Lough Mohra. A steep and occasionally rocky climb leads to the 755m (2478ft) summit of **Knockanaffrin**, which is marked by a cairn. Follow the ridge onwards, which descends in a series of huge steps. There are rocky areas among the heathery slopes, and a fence offers a sure guide in mist, all the way across **The Gap**. The ground suddenly rears up very steeply and the frowning rock face of **Carrigshaneun** is directly above. Outflank this obstacle to one side or the other then pause for breath on a level area above the rugged mound. A gentler slope continues uphill and reaches the broad and stony top of **Carrignagower** at 767m (2516ft), on the very edge of the Comeragh Mountains plateau.

Desperately boggy ground is reached on a broad gap, and it may be necessary to chart circuitous detours around some of the worst parts. Aim for the broad summit often referred to as **Fauscoum** at 792m (2597ft). ◄

> There are some good views from here, but to appreciate them, it is best to wander round the broad and boggy plateau or simply gaze into the rocky depths of Coumshingaun.

Navigating along the broad and boggy crest of the Comeragh Mountains is particularly difficult in mist and foul weather, and there are few features that can readily be identified in this gently undulating wilderness of bog. However, if you walk northwards from Fauscoum, and swing gradually west, a very broad and gentle gap is crossed, followed by a gently swelling moorland hump. Swing more to the south-west and south to cross a rather more obvious boggy gap. A slightly steeper climb leads onto another moorland hump at 744m (2444ft), generally referred to as **Coumalocha**. (Technically, this is the name of a deep corrie, but all too often the summits are nameless!)

Chart a course round the rim of the corrie, but pull back and cross the broad and boggy crest between Coumalocha and **Coumtay**. At this point, pick a course

The rocky headwall of Coumshingaun in the bleak Comeragh Mountains

just a little south of westwards to find a lengthy moorland spur that is the key to the descent. In misty conditions note that there are several changes of direction along this spur, but the idea is to cross the summits of Tooreenmountain and **Milk Hill**; the latter at 451m (1449ft). From the summit of Milk Hill, drop north-west down a steep slope and pick up a track that runs through **Knockavannia** on the way down to a minor road. Follow roads into the **Nire Valley** and continue through the village of **Ballymacarby** to rejoin the course of the East Munster Way at **Fourmilewater**. Keep walking towards **Newcastle** to embark on the next high-level alternative route.

The Irish Coast to Coast Walk

Knockmealdown Mountains

(Days 13 and 14)

Start	Newcastle
Finish	Barnahown
Distance	32km (20 miles)
Map	OSI Discovery 74

The East Munster Way maintains a fairly low profile on the northern slopes of the Knockmealdown Mountains. The Blackwater (Avondhu) Way climbs higher into the mountains later, yet still avoids crossing the summits. The high-level route offered here makes a complete traverse of the Knockmealdown Mountains, taking you from the village of Newcastle all the way to Barnahown above Araglin. It takes the place of *Day 13* and *Day 14* of the waymarked Coast to Coast Walk. The distance covered is about 32km (20 miles), compared to around 40km (25 miles) as the waymarked trails run.

The Knockmealdown Mountains are largely covered in grass and heather, with stony summits and only a few boggy patches along the way. In fact, the range has the reputation of being one of the driest underfoot in Ireland. The upland crest also bears a prominent stone and earth dyke aligned to the county boundary between Co Waterford and the South Riding of Co Tipperary. This offers a useful guide along the crest in misty weather, while in clear weather, views of the surrounding countryside are of course much wider than those obtained down on the forested slopes. A prominent gap in the mountain range is crossed by a road, and this offers a chance to link back into the waymarked trails and descend to Clogheen if accommodation is required. However, this makes for a long detour and it may be easier to climb straight back into the mountains and continue towards the Araglin valley.

Leave the village of **Newcastle** as marked along the East Munster Way, following the road called Bothar na nGall and another road climbing uphill from **Glenboy River**. The East Munster Way later turns right and climbs towards

HIGH-LEVEL ALTERNATIVE ROUTES – KNOCKMEALDOWN MOUNTAINS

Knockroe, but continue to the top of the road instead, crossing a gap and even following the road downhill a short way. Use a forest track on the right, then later leave the forest and climb up the very steep slopes of **Knocknafallia**. The summit rises to 668m (2199ft) and bears a shelter cairn.

Head roughly north-west to descend the stony and heathery slopes of the mountain and cross a gap. Climb straight up the slopes of **Knocknagnauv** to find a stony embankment crossing three gentle swellings. The rise in the middle is the highest, at 655m (2152ft). The stony embankment offers a sure guide onwards, descending to a wide, heathery gap that features a few boggy patches. At that point, it diminishes to become a vague linear mound. Cross the **Rian Bó Phádraig**, or the 'track of St Patrick's cow', at this point. ▶

The stony embankment climbs steeper and steeper up a heathery slope to reach the summit trig point on **Knockmealdown** at 794m (2609ft). Views take in the Galty Mountains, Slievenamon and the Comeragh Mountains, as well as vast tracts of fertile lowland country. This is the highest point in Co Waterford, though the northern slopes fall into Co Tipperary. Follow the stony embankment downhill, noting that it swings suddenly left before reaching **Sugarloaf Hill**. However, a short detour easily includes the 663m (2144ft) summit, which is a notable viewpoint. A well-trodden and very stony path drops steeply downhill alongside the embankment to reach **The Gap** in the middle of the Knockmealdown Mountains. This is crossed by the R668 road, which can be used to leave the route, or connect with the waymarked trails.

Walkers can simply cross over the road and climb straight uphill, but bear in mind that the embankment becomes more difficult to follow. The slope is steep and rugged, with deep heather and rhododendron scrub, but the vegetation cover thins as height is gained and the gradient eases. The embankment dwindles and suddenly veers off to the left, but continue following a groove through the heather to reach a small summit cairn and an outcrop of rock at 630m (2069ft) on Knocknalougha.

This is an ancient pilgrim path that ran from Ardmore on the south coast to the Rock of Cashel further north. It has recently been waymarked as St Declan's Way.

THE IRISH COAST TO COAST WALK

Walkers on top of Knockmealdown the highest point in Co Waterford

Walk southwards from the summit to pick up the line of the embankment again, though now it is little more than a peaty ribbon. As it proceeds towards a gap it looks more like a stony path, but in the end it is necessary to climb straight towards the summit of **Knockshanahullion** without much to aid navigation. The summit bears a trig point at 652m (2153ft) and a large, ancient, bouldery burial cairn has been fashioned into a windbreak shelter.

Head southwards from the summit to pick up the course of the Blackwater (Avondhu) Way and follow it down to a minor road at **Hare's Cross**. The waymarked route soon passes over a gap between low hills, and the high-level route could be continued over **Crow Hill** and Farbreaga (the latter rises to 518m (1706ft)). Joining the waymarked trail again, walk into a network of minor roads and bring the high-level route to a close at **Barnahown**. There is only a solitary farmhouse B&B here, so check in advance if you need accommodation.

Derrynasaggart Mountains
(Days 19 and 20)

Start	Croohig's Cross Roads
Finish	Brewsterfield
Distance	25km (15.5 miles)
Map	OSI Discovery 79

The Blackwater (Duhallow) Way keeps fairly low across the northern slopes of Caherbarnagh, Knocknabro and The Paps. Some walkers might be drawn to consider a high-level walk across those summits, but they should bear in mind that the terrain is quite rugged. Deep heather and awkward tussocky moorland grass could bring you to your knees, though it may be worth the effort to get to know the Derrynasaggart Mountains better. Few walkers know the range, though The Paps are climbed quite regularly. In mist and rain, it is probably best to stay low on the waymarked trail, as the uplands are quite featureless and there are few aids to navigation.

The suggested route follows the waymarked trail from Croohig's Cross Roads, then makes an ascent of Caherbarnagh and aims to stay high over Knocknabro and The Paps. The descent uses an old bog road to reach Islandmore. Unfortunately the main N22 road is the quickest way back onto the Coast to Coast Walk, joined where it passes through Brewsterfield. This stretch isn't waymarked, and in fact there is no waymarked trail available until you reach the Kerry Way at Muckross.

The high-level alternative replaces most of *Day 19* and *Day 20* of the Coast to Coast Walk. The distance covered by the high-level route is around 25km (15.5 miles), which is about the same as staying on the low-level trail. However, the ruggedness of the high-level route ensures that it takes longer to complete.

Follow the Blackwater (Duhallow) Way from **Croohig's Cross Roads**, across Ahaphooca Bridge, and uphill on the rugged slopes of **Gortavehy East**. Leave the waymarked route to climb straight up a steep and rugged slope, reaching a bump at 544m (1785ft) on a broad moorland crest. Swing right to climb further, looking over a cliff to see Gortavehy Lough, then passing a prominent cairn on **Stoukeen**. Keep to the moorland crest, crossing a hump at 627m (2057ft) on the way to the higher summit of **Caherbarnagh** at 681m (2239ft). There is a trig point set well back from a pronounced hollow in the mountainside.

Follow a course south-westwards from the summit to start the descent, then swing more to the west down a steeper slope. This course roughly traces the line of the boundary between Co Cork and Co Kerry, and an old fence aids navigation. There are plenty of boggy patches, areas of heather, and vast expanses of tussocky moorland grass that prove to be quite difficult on the way across a broad gap. Beyond the gap, a gentle slope is actually quite arduous underfoot as the vegetation cover makes walking difficult. There are three summits on the moorland crest of **Knocknabro**. A minor one is crossed around 530m (1740ft) on the way to the highest one at 592m (1958ft).

A descent westwards leads down a steep and rugged slope of deep heather, uneven stony ground and boulders, landing you on a clear track in a deep gap known as the **Sloigeadal**. Walkers who have had enough can turn right and follow the waymarked trail to '**The City**' to continue along the low-level course of the Coast to Coast Walk.

Trig point and ancient cairn on top of one of The Paps high in Co Kerry

HIGH-LEVEL ALTERNATIVE ROUTES – DERRYNASAGGART MOUNTAINS

Walkers who wish to stay high simply cross the gap and make their way towards **The Paps**. There is some deep heather to negotiate above a forest, but this becomes shorter as height is gained. Given the shape of The Paps, which resemble two enormous breasts, the summits aren't really seen until at close quarters. The first summit rises to 694m (2284ft) and bears a prominent and ancient cairn, obviously fashioned to resemble a nipple. Head west across a gap and climb up a heathery slope to the twin summit at 690m (2273ft), which also bears a prominent nipple-cairn as well as a trig point.

After enjoying splendid views ahead to the mountains of Co Kerry, descend directly south, then swing more steeply downhill to the west. Pick up an old track and follow it down a valley to reach **Islandmore**. The busy N22 road can then be followed in the direction of Killarney. The road is uncomfortably busy, but the only way of avoiding it is to look out for old by-passed bends on the way through **Glenflesk** until the Coast to Coast Walk is joined again at **Brewsterfield**.

The twin breasts of The Paps dominate the Derrynasaggart Mountains

The Irish Coast to Coast Walk

MacGillycuddy's Reeks *(Day 22)*

Start	Black Valley Youth Hostel
Finish	Glencar
Distance	26km (16 miles)
Maps	OSI Discovery 78, OSI *MacGillycuddy's Reeks*

The traverse of MacGillycuddy's Reeks is a recognised classic mountain walk and is among the best in the whole of Ireland. It can be brought into play as an alternative to the low-level easy course taken by the Kerry Way through the Black Valley and Bridia Valley. Make no mistake about the high-level nature of this alternative though; it crosses the summits of eight out of the 10 highest mountains in Ireland. The jagged crest includes Carrauntoohil, the highest mountain in Co Kerry, the Province of Munster, and indeed the whole of Ireland.

As the range is close to the Atlantic Ocean and is generally caught in a damp westerly airflow, there are often clouds shrouding the summits. Careful navigation is required in those conditions, although some parts of the ridge bear a well-trodden path. There are many steep and rocky slopes, and one part of the ridge requires basic scrambling skills as you grapple with rocks. Rain can make these rocks particularly slippery and a traverse in foul weather is not recommended.

On a clear day, with ample time at your disposal, this high-level walk makes a fine substitute for half of *Day 22* on the Coast to Coast Walk. If attempted, then it is unlikely that walkers will be able to continue all the way to Glenbeigh, but should think of spending the night in Glencar, perhaps at the Climber's Inn. The distance over the mountains from the Black Valley Youth Hostel to the Climber's Inn is around 26km (16 miles), while the low-level waymarked trail covers 20km (12 miles).

Leave the Kerry Way shortly beyond the **Black Valley Youth Hostel** and follow the rugged road towards the **Gap of Dunloe**. Leave the road before the gap is reached and climb straight up a steep and rugged slope to reach the 464m (1490ft) summit of **Drishana**. This is revealed

HIGH-LEVEL ALTERNATIVE ROUTES – MACGILLYCUDDY'S REEKS

as a mere shoulder of **Cnoc na dTarbh**, which is in turn reached by following a rather blunt, gently graded ridge further uphill. The 655m (2150ft) summit is marked by large blocks of rock. Walk downhill a little to cross a gap, then climb a steeper and more rugged slope to reach the 713m (2398ft) summit of **Cnoc an Bhráca**. A tall cairn stands on top and a line of posts are arranged along its crest.

Walk along the broad crest of Cnoc an Bhráca, crossing a minor rise before descending to a gap. A path crosses the gap and later zig-zags up a steep slope of rock and heather, though there are a couple of level stages where you can pause for breath. The prominent peak of **Cruach Mhór** is crowned by a wall-like structure at 932m (3062ft) with a little niche to hold a statue. The next part of the ridge requires the use of hands as there are shattered rocks that need to be negotiated, as well as some rather exposed steps where care is needed. Pinnacles of rock can generally be passed using an assortment of little paths trodden across steep and rocky slopes. The rocky peak of **The Big Gun** rises to 939m (3080ft).

Keep to the rocky ridge to reach a gap, which in turn is crossed fairly easily. The ridge leading uphill is quite difficult in places, and walkers usually keep to the left to avoid problems. Care is needed on the ascent, then a final steep pull leads up to the 988m (3240ft) summit of **Cnoc na Péiste**. Although you may feel that time has been lost up to this point, with the long ascent and awkward scrambling, things get easier and better progress should be possible. The ridge walk becomes quite simple and a grassy gap beyond Cnoc na Péiste is easily crossed. A short ascent leads to the summit of **Maolán Buí** at 973m (3190ft). A gently graded, but stony ridge runs down to another gap, then there is a very slight ascent to a summit at 926m (3038ft) before the ridge dips down to the next gap. A slightly steeper climb leads onto the grassy summit of **Cnoc an Chuillin**, which bears a cairn at 958m (3141ft). A lengthy descent leads down a steep and stony slope, running out onto a grassy gap. The next climb passes a ruined fence and appears to reach a summit, but continue a little further along the broad and grassy crest to reach the top of **Cnoc na Toinne** at 845m (2776ft). Walk down a grassy ridge leading to a prominent gap at the top of the notorious **Devil's Ladder** – a popular and badly-eroded scree gully often used to access these heights.

Rising above the gap is a broad and stony slope, bearing a clear zig-zag path that climbs all the way to the summit of **Carrauntoohil**. There is no mistaking this point, which bears a prominent metal cross, trig point and shelter cairn. It is the highest point in Ireland at 1039m (3414ft).

If your ascent is blessed with fine weather and clear air, then enjoy the magnificent and extensive views. If time is on your side, then consider a there-and-back scramble along the ridge to neighbouring Beenkeragh as an 'extra'.

Backtrack a little downhill from Carrauntoohil's summit, but take care not to go down to the gap above the **Devil's Ladder**. Instead, head out along the airy ridge towards Caher, where care is required. If the ridge proves too exposed, drop down a little to the south and use a

Climbing the upper stony slopes of Carrauntoohil – the highest in Ireland

HIGH-LEVEL ALTERNATIVE ROUTES – MACGILLYCUDDY'S REEKS

path cutting across the slope. A steep climb from the ridge leads to a stance at 983m (3225ft), from where you can easily walk to the main summit on **Caher** at 1001m (3284ft). Descend roughly south-west along a ridge, swinging more to the south to cross the little hump of **Curraghmore** at 822m (2695ft). Continue the descent south-westwards again, noting how the ridge becomes more roughly vegetated and hummocky. As the ridge begins to swing west, it reaches the top of the **Lack Road** where the waymarked Kerry Way crosses.

Follow the waymarks over the rugged northern side of the gap, and continue past **Lough Acoose** and along the road to the Climber's Inn in **Glencar**. After completing the traverse of MacGillycuddy's Reeks, few walkers would have the time and energy to continue along the Kerry Way to **Glenbeigh** the same day.

View along the rugged ridge of MacGillycuddy's Reeks to Carrauntoohil

Coomasaharn Horseshoe
(Days 22 and 23)

Start	Glencar
Finish	Foilmore
Distance	36km (22 miles)
Maps	OSI Discovery 78 & 83

Coomasaharn is an exceptionally rocky hollow occupied by a large lake in a range of mountains some distance from Glenbeigh. The Kerry Way only takes in the foothills and flanks of those mountains, crossing the Windy Gap to reach Glenbeigh, then crossing the slopes of Drung Hill, Beenmore and Been Hill on the way towards Cahersiveen. Walkers who are prepared to skip Glenbeigh and its facilities could enjoy instead a remote, high-level walk based on the Coomasaharn Horseshoe. Towards the end, you could of course drop down as soon as possible to join the course of the Kerry Way again, but it is better to make the most of the mountain crest by following it all the way to Drung Hill before descending to the waymarked trail. This high-level alternative basically replaces a little of *Day 22* and the first half of *Day 23* on the Coast to Coast Walk. The route measures around 36km (22 miles) if followed along with parts of the Kerry Way from Glencar to the Windy Gap and from Drung Hill to Foilmore. The low-level waymarked Kerry Way on its own measures only 21km (13 miles) between Glencar and Foilmore.

Glencar to **Glenbeigh**, but switch to the course of the high-level alternative from the top of the **Windy Gap**. A short climb leads up heathery slopes to the summit of **Coolroe** at 414m (1361ft). Descend southwards towards a hummocky gap, then climb in stages, hampered by long grass and heather, as well as boggy patches, along the broad moorland crest of **Beenreagh**. The summit rises to 495m (1628ft). A short, but fairly steep descent lands on a broad gap, then a longer and steeper pull leads up to the 607m (1998ft) summit of **Macklaun**. Beyond Macklaun lies a long and broad ridge that draws walkers

HIGH-LEVEL ALTERNATIVE ROUTES – COOMASAHARN HORSESHOE

The view down on Coomasaharn while negotiating the horseshoe walk

THE IRISH COAST TO COAST WALK

This wall and ditch proves to be a useful guide over the next few summits, especially in mist, so walk alongside it and become familiar with its construction. Look over the edge of a steep slope into the rocky confines of Coomasaharn.

onwards, then a long spur leads uphill and round the precipitous slopes of **Coomeeneragh**, to gain the 715m (2350ft) summit of **Meenteog**.

Follow the broad moorland slope downhill from Meenteog and trace an old boundary wall and ditch across a broad gap. ◀ The wall and ditch runs uphill, but you will find that a boggy ditch and a line of fenceposts actually cross the 772m (2541ft) summit of **Coomacarrea**. The boundary ditch can be traced downhill, then a fence accompanies it across the next gap. The line of the ditch becomes vague further along, but it can be traced round the head of Coomasaharn on the upper slopes of **Teermoyle Mountain**. A simple detour allows the 760m (2442ft) summit to be visited, which is mostly peaty with rashes of stones.

The boundary mound and ditch leads down a broad slope of stones and bare peat on the northern side of Teermoyle Mountain. A fence later runs across a broad gap and you can look down into the rugged hollow of Coomaglaslaw. The fence turns off to the left, but keep following the stony mound uphill and the summit of **Mullaghnarakill** is reached. The highest point is 665m (2182ft) and there are large slabs of rock around. The boundary ditch runs across the eastern slopes of **Been Hill**, crossing a couple of streams falling into Coomacronia. ◀

If you wish to visit the summit of Been Hill, at 651m (2130ft), then make a detour westwards to include it.

Beenmore is the next summit in line and a stony mound leads straight up a steep and heathery slope. A shelter-cairn is passed on the way uphill to the 669m (2199ft) summit, marked by a cairn. Continue along a narrow, heathery ridge which bears a path leading straight towards **Drung Hill** – the last summit on the circuit. Views from the trig point and cairn at 640m (2104ft) take in ranges of mountains on both the Iveragh and Dingle peninsulas of Co Kerry. By heading roughly westwards, the very steep descent gradually eases and the rugged ground gives way to a track. Turn left and follow this track, which is part of the Kerry Way, across the lower slopes of the hill. ◀

The route can be followed towards Foilmore, where B&B accommodation can be found if there is no time to continue all the way to Cahersiveen.

This is the last of the high-level alternative routes and the remainder of the Irish Coast to Coast Walk stays at a low level to reach a conclusion out on **Valentia Island**.

APPENDIX A
Glossary of Common Irish Words

Most of the placenames that appear on Ordnance Survey of Ireland maps are Anglicised versions of Irish placenames, which themselves may have been in use for over 2000 years. Sometimes, the names have become so corrupted that the original meaning has been lost. However, most Irish placenames are often highly descriptive, so that even a curious-looking name like *Knockmealdown* can be broken down into *Cnoc, Maol* and *Donn*, or 'bald, brown hill', which describes Knockmealdown perfectly!

As the 1:50,000 Ordnance Survey of Ireland Discovery maps were rolled out, it became a policy to include as many original Irish placenames as possible alongside the Anglicised versions. The following list can be used to translate some of the Irish placenames into English, if only to see how closely those names still fit the landscape features to which they were originally applied.

Irish Form	Anglicised Form	Meaning
Abhainn	Owen	River
Achadh	Augha	Field
Aill	Ail/all	Cliff
Ard	Ard	Height
Ath	Ath	Ford
Baile	Bally	Town/townland
Bán	Baun/bawn	White
Barr	Bar	Top
Beag	Beg	Small
Bealach	Ballagh	Pass/gap
Beann	Ben	Mountain
Bearna	Barna	Pass/gap
Beith	Beigh	Birch
Bóthar	Boher	Road
Bótharín	Bohreen	Lane
Breac	Brack	Speckled
Buaile	Booley	Summer pasture
Buí	Boy	Yellow
Bun	Bun	Foot/end

THE IRISH COAST TO COAST WALK

Irish Form	Anglicised Form	Meaning
Caiseal	Cashel	Stone fort
Carn	Carn	Cairn
Carraig	Carrick	Rock
Cathair	Caher	Stone fort
Ceann	Ken	Head
Ceapach	Cappagh	Plot of land
Cill	Kill	Church
Cloch	Clogh	Stone
Cluain	Cloon/clon	Meadow
Cnoc	Knock	Hill
Coill	Kil	Wood
Coire	Corry	Corrie
Cor	Cor	Round hill
Corrán	Carraun	Sickle
Cruach	Croagh	Steep-sided hill
Cúm	Coom	Corrie
Dearg	Derg	Red
Doire	Derry	Oak
Donn	Dun/doon	Brown
Druim	Drum	Rounded ridge
Dubh	Duff/doo	Black
Dún	Dun/doon	Earth fort
Eas	Ass/ess	Waterfall
Eisk	Esk	Steep gully
Fionn	Fin/finn	Fair/clear
Fraioch	Freagh	Heath
Gaoith	Gwee/gee	Wind
Garbh	Garriff	Rough
Glas	Glas	Green/grey
Gleann	Glen	Valley
Gorm	Gorm	Blue
Gort	Gort	Field
Inbhear	Inver	River mouth
Inis	Inish	Island
Leac	Lack	Flagstone
Leacht	Lack	Large cairn
Liath	Leagh	Grey

Appendix A – Glossary of Common Irish Words

Irish Form	Anglicised Form	Meaning
Loch	Lough	Lake
Log	Log/lug	Hollow
Machaire	Maghery	Plain
Maol	Mweel/meal	Bald
Mór	More	Big
Muc	Muck	Pig
Muillean	Mullin	Mill
Mullach	Mullagh	Summit
Poll	Poll/poul	Hole/cave
Rath	Rath	Earth fort
Rí	Ree	King
Rinn	Rinn	Headland
Ruadh	Roe	Ruddy/red
Scairbh	Scarriff	Shallow ford
Sceilig	Skellig	Rock
Sean	Shan	Old
Sídh	Shee	Fairy mound
Sliabh	Slieve	Mountain
Slí	Slee/slea	Way
Spinc	Spink	Point
Srón	Sron	Nose
Stuaic	Stook	Pinnacle
Suí	See	Seat
Taobh	Tave	Side
Tír	Teer	Land
Tobar	Tubber	Well
Torc	Torc	Wild boar

Additionally, particles such as *an* or *na* can have the meaning of 'the' or 'of the'. Words ending in *ín* or *een* have the meaning of 'little', so that *Stuaicín* or *Stookeen* would mean 'little pinnacle'.

APPENDIX B
Irish Coast to Coast Walk Accommodation List

The intention of this list is to highlight accommodation that is close to the Irish Coast to Coast Walk, or can be reached by short diversions, especially in areas where accommodation may be sparse. Some addresses are 'approved' by Fáilte Ireland (Irish Tourist Board) and can be found on their lists. Others are not 'approved', but walkers may be keen to know about them if they are close to the route. Only the most basic contact details are given, so if you need particular facilities, please enquire when first making contact. Many of these addresses, particularly in remote locations, are willing to pick up and drop off walkers by prior arrangement. Again, ask about this in advance if you think you will need assistance. Irish hospitality is legendary, but it has its limits!

Bear in mind that once a booking has been made, a contract exists between you and the proprietor. Please ensure that you give due notice if you have to cancel, or otherwise change your arrangements. Walkers who fail to show for accommodation stand to lose any deposit they have paid. Worse, failure to show could lead to the emergency services being notified.

DUBLIN
Ireland's capital city contains numerous hotels, guesthouses, B&Bs and hostels. Personal callers are welcome to book their accommodation at the Dublin tourism office in St Andrew's Church on Suffolk Street, just off-route from Grafton Street. Alternatively, you can make credit card bookings (tel 01–8200394).

KNOCKREE
Knockree Youth Hostel, tel 01–2864036
Oaklawn House, Glaskenny, tel 01–2860493

ENNISKERRY (Addresses 3–5km off-route)
Powerscourt Arms Hotel, tel 01–2828903
Ferndale, tel 01–2863518
Corner House, tel 01–2860149
Summerhill House Hotel, tel 01–2867928
Coillte, Enniskerry Demesne, tel 01–2766614
Cherbury, Monastery, tel 01–2828679

POWERSCOURT (Address 2km off-route)
Coolakay House, tel 01–2862423

ROUNDWOOD (Addresses 2–3km off-route)
Tochar House, tel 01–2818247
The Coach House, tel 01–2818157
Woodside, tel 01–2818195
Ballinacor House, tel 01–2818168
Oakwell, tel 01-2818332
Riverbank, tel 01-2818117
Roundwood Campsite, tel 01–2818163

OLDBRIDGE
Wicklow Way Lodge, tel 01–2818489

ANNAMOE (Address 2km off-route)
Carmel's, tel 0404–45297
Bracken, tel 0404–45300

LARAGH (Addresses 1–2km off-route)
Laragh Mountain View Lodge, tel 0404–45302
Glendale, tel 0404–45410
Pinewood Lodge, tel 0404–45437
Dunroamin House, tel 0404–45487
Avalon, tel 0404–45331
Mountainview, tel 0404–45485
Oakview, tel 0404–45453
Gleann Ailbhe, tel 0404–45236
Lynham's of Laragh, tel 0404–45345
Tudor Lodge, tel 0404–45554

GLENDALOUGH
Valeview, tel 0404–45292
Glendalough Hotel, tel 0404–45135
Glendalough Youth Hostel, tel 0404–45690

GLENMALURE
Glenmalure Lodge, tel 0404–46188
Coolalingo, tel 0404–46583

AUGHRIM (Address 8km off-route)
Butlers Byrne, near Aughrim, tel 0402-36644

MOYNE (Addresses 1km off-route)
Jigsaw Cottage, tel 0508-71071
Kyle Farmhouse, tel 0508-71341

TINAHELY (Addresses 1–2km off-route)
Rosbane Farmhouse, tel 0402-38100
Murphy's Hotel, tel 0402-38109
Orchard House, Coolruss, tel 0402-38264
Ramblers Way, Glenphilipeen, tel 0402-38324
Sunindale House, tel 0402-38170

CROSSBRIDGE
Ashfield, tel 0402-38146

KILQUIGGIN (Address 2km off-route)
Aspen Lodge, Killabeg, tel 0503-56120

SHILLELAGH (Addresses 3km off-route)
The Avalon, tel 055-29149
The Olde Shillelagh, tel 055-29113
Park Lodge, Park, tel 055-29140

CLONEGAL
Clonegal House, tel 054-77293
An Ruadan, tel 054-77927

KILDAVIN (Address 3km off-route)
Sherwood Park House, Ballon, tel 0503-59117

TOMDUFF
Moongate, tel 0503-73669

BORRIS
Step House, Main Street, tel 0503-73209
Mitchela, Main Street Tel 0503-73729

APPENDIX B – IRISH COAST TO COAST WALK ACCOMMODATION LIST

GRAIGUENAMANAGH
Anchor Bar, Main Street, tel 0503–24576
Water Side Guest House, The Quay, tel 0503–24246
Old Mill House, Mill Street, tel 0503–24769

INISTIOGE
Norebridge House, tel 056–7758158
Nore Valley Villa, tel 056–7758418
Bank House, tel 056–7758588
Woodstock Arms, tel 056–7758440
Ashville, Kilmacshane, tel 056–7758460

LUKESWELL
Hillview Farmhouse, tel 051–898221

MULLINAVAT
The Rising Sun, Main Street, tel 051–898173
St Anthony's, Main Street, tel 051–898165

PILTOWN
Kildalton House, tel 051–643196
Fanningstown House, tel 051–643535

CARRICK-ON-SUIR
Cedarfield House, Waterford Road, tel 051–640164
Hillcrest, Greenhill Close, tel 051–640847
Carraig Hotel, Main Street, tel 051–641455
Bell & Salmon Arms, Main Street, tel 051–645555
The Vic, Sean Kelly Square, tel 051–641476
Fatima House, John Street, tel 051–640298
An Caislean, Waterford Rd, Carrick Beg, 051–640508
Caravan & Camping Park, Kilkenny Road, tel 051–640461

KILSHEELAN
Nagles Bar, tel 052–33496

HARNEY'S CROSS
Powers the Pot Hostel & Campsite, tel 052–23085

The Irish Coast to Coast Walk

CLONMEL
Clonmel Arms Hotel, Sarsfield Street, tel 052–21233
Hotel Minella, Coleville Road, tel 052–22388
Hearns Hotel, Parnell Street, tel 052–21611
Mulcahy's Hotel, Gladstone Street, tel 052–25054
Fennessy's Hotel, Gladstone Street, tel 052–23680
Mr Bumbles, Kickham Street, tel 052–29188
Brighton House, Brighton Place, tel 052–23665
Raheen House, Raheen Road, tel 052–22140
Knockainey, Coleville Road, tel 052–23148
Ashbourne, Coleville Road, tel 052–22307
Hillcourt, Marlfield Road, tel 052–21029
Benuala, Marlfield Road, tel 052–22158
Wonderland, Marlfield Road, tel 052–21446
Amberville, Glenconnor Road, tel 052–21470
Lissarda, Old Spa Road, tel 052–22593

FOURMILEWATER
Glasha, tel 052–36108

NEWCASTLE (Addresses 3km off-route)
River Valley, tel 052–36105
Kilmaneen Farmhouse, Kilmaneen, tel 052–36231

CLOGHEEN
Two Rivers, Main Street, tel 052–65499
Parsons Green Campsite, tel 052–65290
Ballyboy House, tel 052–65297

ARAGLIN
Radhairc Alainn, Barnahown, tel 058–50007

KEANE'S CROSS
Keane's Cross, tel 025–27526

KILWORTH
Fuchsia House Hostel, tel 025–27565

KILCRUMPER
Danmar House, Ballyhindon, tel 025–31786

Appendix B – Irish Coast to Coast Walk Accommodation List

FERMOY
Virginia House, Church Place, tel 025–31704
The Townhouse, tel 025–33029
The Grand Hotel, tel 025–31444
Avona, Pike Road, tel 025–32195
Ardvarna, Duntaheen Road, tel 025–31858
Palm Rise, Duntaheen, tel 025–31386
Ardvarna, Duntaheen Road, tel 025–31858
Avonmore, Mallow Road, tel 025–32568
Ard na Houn, Mallow Road, tel 025–32895
Ashfield House, Castlehyde, tel 025–31226
Blackwater Caravan & Camping, tel 025–32147

BALLYHOOLY (Address 1.5km off-route)
The Old Train House, tel 025–39337

BEARFOREST (Address 3km off-route)
Rivervale Lodge, tel 022–22218

MALLOW (Addresses 3–4km off-route)
Hibernian Hotel, Main Street, tel 022–21588
Mallow Park Hotel. Main Street, tel 022–21527
Cortigan House, Golf Course Road, tel 022–22770
Longueville House, tel 022–47156
Ard-na-Laoi, Bathview, tel 022–22317
Oaklands, Springwood, tel 022–21227
Riverside House, Navigation Road, tel 022–42761
Hill Top View, Navigation Road, tel 022–21491
Leadon, Navigation Road, tel 022–21661
Ackworth, Navigation Road, tel 022–21325
Annabella Lodge, tel 022–43991

BURNFORT (Address 4km off-route)
Windwood, tel 022–29417

LAHARAN CROSS ROADS (Address 6km off-route)
Ard na Coille, Glounminane, tel 022–47482

BANTEER (Addresses 15km off-route)
Agherton Lodge, Clonmeen, tel 029–56388

The Irish Coast to Coast Walk

Roche's Country House, Rossnalee, tel 029–56125
Duhallow Park Hotel, tel 029–56152

GEARAROE
Geararoe, tel 029–70099

MILLSTREET (Addresses 2km off-route)
The Laurels, Minor Row, tel 029–70090
Knockdrish, Drishane Road, tel 029–70617
Drishane Lodge, tel 029–70184

BALLINATONA (Address 2km off-route)
Ballinatona Farm House, tel 029–70213

BALLYDALY (Address 2km off-route)
Robins Nest, tel 029–70447

RATHMORE (Address 8km off-route)
Fáilte, Shinnagh, tel 064–58178

MINISH (Addresses 2km off-route)
Dunbery House, tel 064–37477
River Valley Farmhouse, tel 064–32411

MUCKROSS
Valley View, Lough Guitane Road, tel 064–31206
Forest Haven, Lough Guitane Road, tel 064–33757
Kiltrasna Farm, Lough Guitane Road, tel 064–31643
Cill-Ide, Muckross Church Road, tel 064–33339
Torc Falls, Lough Guitane Road, tel 064–33566
Muckross Park Hotel, tel 064–31938

KILLARNEY
There is a huge amount of accommodation of all types off-route at Killarney, including several addresses along Muckross Road on the approach to town. Contact the tourist information office for full details or to make a booking (tel 064–31633).

BLACK VALLEY
Hillcrest Farmhouse, tel 064–34702

Black Valley Youth Hostel, tel 064–34712
Shamrock Farmhouse, tel 064–34714

GLENCAR
Lough Acoose House, tel 066–9760105
Blackstones House, tel 066–9760164
The Climber's Inn, tel 066–9760101

GLENBEIGH
Liosderrig House, tel 066–9768717
Oaktree Lodge, tel 066–9768606
Towers Hotel, tel 066–9768212
The Village House, tel 066–9768128
Chipchase House, tel 066–9768657
Ocean Wave, tel 066–9768249
Glencurragh House, tel 066–9768133
Forest View, tel 066–9768140

MOUNTAIN STAGE
Mountain View, tel 066–9768541

FOILMORE
Fransal House, tel 066–9472997
Failte Farmhouse, Derrymore, tel 066–9472425

CAHERSIVEEN
Iveragh Heights, Carhan Road, tel 066–9472545
Mount Rivers, Carhan Road, tel 066–9472509
O'Shea's, Church Street, tel 066–9472402
Castleview, Valentia Road, tel 066–9472252
San Antoine, Valentia Road, tel 066–9472521
Cul Draiochta, Valentia Road, tel 066–9473141
Avoca Lodge, Garranearagh, tel 066–9473947
Sive Independent Hostel, tel 066–9472717
Mannix Point Camping & Caravan Site, tel 066–9472806

REENARD POINT
Sea Breeze, tel 066–9472609
Ocean View, tel 066–9472261
Seafront Farmhouse, tel 066–9472357

The Irish Coast to Coast Walk

Ferryview, tel 066-9472052

KNIGHTSTOWN
Royal Pier Hotel & Hostel, tel 066-9476144
Valentia Harbour, tel 066-9476204
Spring Acre, tel 066-9476141
Altazamuth, tel 066-9476300
Glenreen Heights, tel 066-9476241
Valentia Island Youth Hostel, tel 066-9476154
Combe Bank House Hostel, tel 066-9476111

GLANLEAM
Glanleam House, tel 066-9476176

PORTMAGEE
Carraig Liath (on Valentia Island), tel 066-9476344
The Moorings, tel 066-9477108
The Waterfront, tel 066-9477208
Reen Coast, Reencaheragh, tel 066-9477247

If phoning from outside Ireland, dial 00-353, then drop the first zero from the area code and continue dialling the rest of the number. If using a mobile phone in Ireland, bear in mind that a signal may not be available in remote or mountainous areas.

APPENDIX C
Route Summary Table

This route summary offers a further breakdown of distances to supplement those quoted at the introduction to each daily stage. Careful use of a series of intermediate breaks allows walkers to chop and change the route schedule, maybe walking a bit more one day, then cutting a longer stage short. Most of the stages listed below are within reach of accommodation or bus services, but read each day's route description carefully as you may need to organise for a pick-up in advance at some of the more remote places. Throughout the summary, distances for each of the stages are given in kilometres and miles, with the cumulative totals at the end of each row.

	Section Distance	Cumulative Distance
Stage 1: The Wicklow Way		
Dublin to Marlay Park	11km (7 miles)	11km (7 miles)
Marlay Park to Glencullen	11km (7 miles)	22km (14 miles)
Glencullen to Knockree	9km (5.5 miles)	31km (19.5 miles)
Knockree to Baltynanima	18km (11 miles)	49km (30.5 miles)
Baltynanima to Laragh	10km (6 miles)	59km (36.5 miles)
Laragh to Glendalough	4km (2.5 miles)	63km (39 miles)
Glendalough to Glenmalure	13km (8 miles)	76km (47 miles)
Glenmalure to Moyne	21km (13 miles)	97km (60 miles)
Moyne to Tinahely	15km (9.5 miles)	112km (69.5 miles)
Tinahely to Kilquiggan	13km (8 miles)	125km (77.5 miles)
Kilquiggan to Clonegal	21km (13 miles)	146km (90.5 miles)
Stage 2: The South Leinster Way		
Clonegal to Tomduff	19km (11.5 miles)	165km (102 miles)
Tomduff to Borris	7km (4.5 miles)	172km (106.5 miles)
Borris to Graiguenamanagh	12km (7.5 miles)	184km (114 miles)
Graiguenamanagh to Inistioge	16km (10 miles)	200km (124 miles)
Inistioge to Lukeswell	26km (16.25 miles)	226km (140.25 miles)
Lukeswell to Mullinavat	4km (2.5 miles)	230km (142.75 miles)
Mullinavat to Piltown	15km (9 miles)	245km (152 miles)
Piltown to Carrick-on-Suir	8km (5 miles)	253km (157 miles)

The Irish Coast to Coast Walk

	Section Distance	Cumulative Distance
Stage 3: The East Munster Way		
Carrick-on-Suir to Kilsheelan	12km (7.5 miles)	265km (164.5 miles)
Kilsheelan to Clonmel	18km (11 miles)	283km (175.5 miles)
Clonmel to Fourmilewater	16km (10 miles)	299km (185.5 miles)
Fourmilewater to Newcastle	5km (3 miles)	304km (188.5 miles)
Newcastle to Goatenbridge	10km (6 miles)	314km (194.5 miles)
Goatenbridge to Clogheen	12km 7.5 miles)	326km (202 miles)
Stage 4: The Blackwater (Avondhu) Way		
Clogheen to Araglin	20km (12.5 miles)	346km (214.5 miles)
Araglin to Kilworth	20km (12.5 miles)	366km (227 miles)
Kilworth to Fermoy	7km (4.5 miles)	373km (231.5 miles)
Fermoy to Ballyhooly	14km (8.5 miles)	387km (240 miles)
Ballyhooly to Killavullen	12km (7.5 miles)	399km (247.5 miles)
Killavullen to Ballynamona	15km (9.5 miles)	414km (257 miles)
Ballynamona to Bweeng	18km (11 miles)	432km (268 miles)
Stage 5: The Blackwater (Duhallow) Way		
Bweeng to Millstreet Country Park	30km (19 miles)	462km (287 miles)
Millstreet Country Park to Millstreet	10km (6 miles)	472km (293 miles)
Millstreet to Ballydaly	8km (5 miles)	480km (298 miles)
Ballydaly to Shrone	14km (9 miles)	494km (307 miles)
Shrone to Headford	8km (5 miles)	502km (312 miles)
Headford to Muckross	12km (7.5 miles)	514km (319.5 miles)
Stage 6: The Kerry Way		
Muckross to Black Valley	20km (12.5 miles)	534km (332 miles)
Black Valley to Glencar	23km (14 miles)	557 (346 miles)
Glencar to Glenbeigh	13km (8 miles)	570km (354 miles)
Glenbeigh to Cahersiveen	22km (13.75 miles)	592km (367.75 miles)
Mountain Stage to Cahersiveen	6km (3.75 miles)	598km (371.5 miles)
Cahersiveen to Knightstown	5km (3 miles)	603km (374.5 miles)
Knightstown to Portmagee	20km (12.5 miles)	623km (387 miles)

NOTES

SAVE £££'s with

tgo
THE GREAT OUTDOORS

Britain's leading monthly magazine for the dedicated walker. To find out how much you can save by subscribing call

0141 302 7744

HILLWALKING • BACKPACKING • TREKKING • SCRAMBLING

It's time to Climb!

CLIMB
MAGAZINE

Climb Magazine features authoritive articles from well respected writers, with stunning photography, great covermounts, competitions and giveaways - every month

Available from Newsagents, specialist gear shops or by subscription.

Call the subscription hotline on 01536 382563
www.climbmagazine.com

Greenshires Publishing, Telford Way, Kettering, Northants NN16 8UN
Tel: 01536 382500 Fax: 01536 382501
Email:info@climbmagazine.com

Get ready for take off

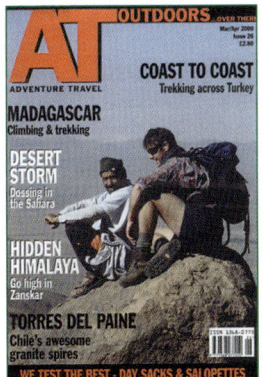

Adventure Travel helps you to go outdoors over there

More ideas, information, advice and entertaining features on overseas trekking, walking and backpacking than any other magazine - guaranteed.

Available from good newsagents or by subscription - 6 issues £15

Adventure Travel Magazine T:01789-488166

LISTING OF CICERONE GUIDES

NORTHERN ENGLAND
LONG-DISTANCE TRAILS
The Dales Way
The Reiver's Way
The Alternative Coast to Coast
The Coast to Coast Walk
The Pennine Way
Hadrian's Wall Path
The Teesdale Way

FOR COLLECTORS OF SUMMITS
The Relative Hills of Britain
Mts England & Wales Vol 2 – England
Mts England & Wales Vol 1 – Wales

BRITISH CYCLE GUIDES
The Cumbria Cycle Way
Lands End to John O'Groats – Cycle Guide
On the Ruffstuff: 84 Bike Rides in North England
Rural Rides No.1 – West Surrey
Rural Rides No.2 – East Surrey
South Lakeland Cycle Rides
Border Country Cycle Routes
Lancashire Cycle Way

CANOE GUIDES
Canoeist's Guide to the North-East

LAKE DISTRICT AND MORECAMBE BAY
Coniston Copper Mines
Scrambles in the Lake District
More Scrambles in the Lake District
Walks in Silverdale and Arnside AONB
Short Walks in Lakeland 1 – South
Short Walks in Lakeland 2 – North
Short Walks in Lakeland 3 – West
The Tarns of Lakeland Vol 1 – West
The Tarns of Lakeland Vol 2 – East
The Cumbria Way & Allerdale Ramble
Winter Climbs in the Lake District
Roads and Tracks of the Lake District
The Lake District Angler's Guide
Rain or Shine – Walking in the Lake District
Rocky Rambler's Wild Walks
An Atlas of the English Lakes

NORTH-WEST ENGLAND
Walker's Guide to the Lancaster Canal
Walking in Cheshire
Family Walks in the Forest Of Bowland
Walks in Ribble Country
Historic Walks in Cheshire
Walking in Lancashire
Walks in Lancashire Witch Country
The Ribble Way

THE ISLE OF MAN
Walking on the Isle of Man
The Isle of Man Coastal Path

PENNINES AND NORTH-EAST ENGLAND
Walks in the Yorkshire Dales – Vol 1
Walking in the South Pennines
Walking in the North Pennines
The Yorkshire Dales
Walks in the North York Moors – Vol 1
Walks in the North York Moors – Vol 2
Walking in the Wolds
Waterfall Walks – Teesdale and High Pennines
Walking in County Durham
Yorkshire Dales Angler's Guide
Backpacker's Britain – Northern England
Walks in Dales Country
Historic Walks in North Yorkshire
South Pennine Walks
Walking in Northumberland

DERBYSHIRE, PEAK DISTRICT, EAST MIDLANDS
High Peak Walks
White Peak Walks Northern Dales
White Peak Walks Southern Dales
White Peak Way
The Viking Way
Star Family Walks Peak District & South Yorkshire
Walking In Peakland
Historic Walks in Derbyshire

WALES AND WELSH BORDERS
Ascent of Snowdon
Welsh Winter Climbs
Hillwalking in Wales – Vol 1
Hillwalking in Wales – Vol 2
Scrambles in Snowdonia
Hillwalking in Snowdonia
The Ridges of Snowdonia
Hereford & the Wye Valley
Walking Offa's Dyke Path
The Brecon Beacons
Lleyn Peninsula Coastal Path
Anglesey Coast Walks
The Shropshire Way
Spirit Paths of Wales
Glyndwr's Way
The Pembrokeshire Coastal Path
Walking in Pembrokeshire
The Shropshire Hills – A Walker's Guide
Backpacker's Britain Vol 2 – Wales

MIDLANDS
The Cotswold Way
West Midlands Rock
The Grand Union Canal Walk
Walking in Oxfordshire
Walking in Warwickshire
Walking in Worcestershire
Walking in Staffordshire
Heart of England Walks

SOUTHERN ENGLAND
The Wealdway & the Vanguard Way
Exmoor & the Quantocks
Walking in the Chilterns
Walks in Kent Book 2
Two Moors Way
Walking in Dorset
Walking in Cornwall
A Walker's Guide to the Isle of Wight
Walking in Devon
Walking in Somerset
The Thames Path
Channel Island Walks
Walking in Buckinghamshire
The Isles of Scilly
Walking in Hampshire
Walking in Bedfordshire
The Lea Valley Walk
Walking in Berkshire
The Definitive Guide to Walking in London
The Greater Ridgeway
Walking on Dartmoor
The South West Coast Path
Walking in Sussex
The North Downs Way
The South Downs Way

SCOTLAND
Scottish Glens 1 – Cairngorm Glens
Scottish Glens 2 – Atholl Glens
Scottish Glens 3 – Glens of Rannoch
Scottish Glens 4 – Glens of Trossach
Scottish Glens 5 – Glens of Argyll
Scottish Glens 6 – The Great Glen
Scottish Glens 7 – The Angus Glens
Scottish Glens 8 – Knoydart to Morvern
Scottish Glens 9 – The Glens of Ross-shire
Scrambles in Skye
The Island of Rhum
Torridon – A Walker's Guide
Ski Touring in Scotland
Walking the Galloway Hills
Walks from the West Highland Railway
Border Pubs & Inns – A Walkers' Guide
Walks in the Lammermuirs
Scrambles in Lochaber
Walking in the Hebrides
Central Highlands: 6 Long Distance Walks
Walking in the Isle Of Arran
Walking in the Lowther Hills
North to the Cape
The Border Country – A Walker's Guide
Winter Climbs – Cairngorms
The Speyside Way
Winter Climbs – Ben Nevis & Glencoe
The Isle of Skye, A Walker's Guide

The West Highland Way
Scotland's Far North
Walking the Munros Vol 1 –
  Southern, Central
Walking the Munros Vol 2 –
  Northern & Cairngorms
Scotland's Far West
Walking in the Cairngorms

IRELAND
The Mountains of Ireland
Irish Coastal Walks
The Irish Coast to Coast

INTERNATIONAL CYCLE GUIDES
The Way of St James – Le Puy to
  Santiago cyclist's guide
The Danube Cycle Way
Cycle Tours in Spain
Cycling the River Loire – The Way
  of St Martin

WALKING AND TREKKING
IN THE ALPS
Grand Tour of Monte Rosa Vol 1
Grand Tour of Monte Rosa Vol 2
Walking in the Alps (all Alpine
  areas)
100 Hut Walks in the Alps
Chamonix to Zermatt
Tour of Mont Blanc
Alpine Ski Mountaineering
  Vol 1 Western Alps
Alpine Ski Mountaineering
  Vol 2 Eastern Alps
Snowshoeing: Techniques and
  Routes in the Western Alps
Alpine Points of View

FRANCE, BELGIUM AND
LUXEMBOURG
The Tour of the Queyras
Rock Climbs in the Verdon
RLS (Robert Louis Stevenson) Trail
Walks in Volcano Country
French Rock
Walking the French Gorges
Rock Climbs Belgium &
  Luxembourg
Tour of the Oisans: GR54
Walking in the Tarentaise and
  Beaufortain Alps
The Brittany Coastal Path
Walking in the Haute Savoie
Walking in the Ardennes
Tour of the Vanoise
Walking in the Languedoc
GR20 Corsica – The High Level
  Route
The Ecrins National Park
Walking the French Alps: GR5
Walking in the Cevennes
Vanoise Ski Touring
Walking in Provence
Walking on Corsica
Mont Blanc Walks
Walking in the Cathar region
  of south west France
Walking in the Dordogne

PYRENEES AND FRANCE / SPAIN
Rock Climbs in the Pyrenees
Walks & Climbs in the Pyrenees
he GR10 Trail: Through the
  French Pyrenees
The Way of St James –
  Le Puy to the Pyrenees
The Way of St James –
  Pyrenees-Santiago-Finisterre
Through the Spanish Pyrenees
  GR11
The Pyrenees – World's Mountain
  Range Guide
The Pyrenean Haute Route
Walking in Andorra

SPAIN AND PORTUGAL
Picos de Europa – Walks & Climbs
Andalusian Rock Climbs
The Mountains of Central Spain
Costa Blanca Rock
Walking in Mallorca
Rock Climbs in Majorca,
  Ibiza & Tenerife
Costa Blanca Walks Vol 1
Costa Blanca Walks Vol 2
Walking in Madeira
Via de la Plata (Seville To Santiago)
Walking in the Cordillera
  Cantabrica
Walking in the Canary Islands 1
  West
Walking in the Canary Islands 2
  East
Walking in the Sierra Nevada

SWITZERLAND
The Jura: Walking the High Route &
  Ski Traverses
Walking in Ticino, Switzerland
Central Switzerland –
  A Walker's Guide
The Bernese Alps
Walking in the Valais
Alpine Pass Route
Walks in the Engadine, Switzerland

GERMANY AND AUSTRIA
Klettersteig Scrambles in
  Northern Limestone Alps
King Ludwig Way
Walking in the Salzkammergut
Walking in the Black Forest
Walking in the Harz Mountains
Walking in the Bavarian Alps
Germany's Romantic Road
Mountain Walking in Austria
Walking the River Rhine Trail
Trekking in the Stubai Alps
Trekking in the Zillertal Alps

SCANDINAVIA
Walking In Norway
The Pilgrim Road to Nidaros
  (St Olav's Way)

EASTERN EUROPE
Trekking in the Caucausus
The High Tatras
The Mountains of Romania
Walking in Hungary

CROATIA AND SLOVENIA
Walks in the Julian Alps
Walking in Croatia

ITALY
Italian Rock
Walking in the Central Italian Alps
Central Apennines of Italy
Walking in Italy's Gran Paradiso
Long Distance Walks in Italy's Gran
  Paradiso
Walking in Sicily
Shorter Walks in the Dolomites
Treks in the Dolomites
Via Ferratas of the Italian
  Dolomites Vol 1
Via Ferratas of the Italian
  Dolomites Vol 2
Walking in the Dolomites
Walking in Tuscany
Trekking in the Apennines

OTHER MEDITERRANEAN
COUNTRIES
The Mountains of Greece
Climbs & Treks in the Ala Dag
  (Turkey)
The Mountains of Turkey
Treks & Climbs Wadi Rum, Jordan
Jordan – Walks, Treks, Caves etc.
Crete – The White Mountains
Walking in Palestine
Walking in Malta

AFRICA
Climbing in the Moroccan Anti-Atlas
Trekking in the Atlas Mountains
Kilimanjaro

NORTH AMERICA
The Grand Canyon &
  American South West
Walking in British Columbia
The John Muir Trail

SOUTH AMERICA
Aconcagua

HIMALAYAS – NEPAL, INDIA
Langtang, Gosainkund &
  Helambu: A Trekkers' Guide
Garhwal & Kumaon –
  A Trekkers' Guide
Kangchenjunga – A Trekkers' Guide
Manaslu – A Trekkers' Guide
Everest – A Trekkers' Guide
Annapurna – A Trekker's Guide
Bhutan – A Trekker's Guide
  DELAYED

AUSTRALIA AND NEW ZEALAND
Classic Tramps in New Zealand

TECHNIQUES AND EDUCATION
The Adventure Alternative
Rope Techniques
Snow & Ice Techniques
Mountain Weather
Beyond Adventure
The Hillwalker's Manual
The Book of the Bivvy
Outdoor Photography
The Hillwalker's Guide to
  Mountaineering
Map and Compass

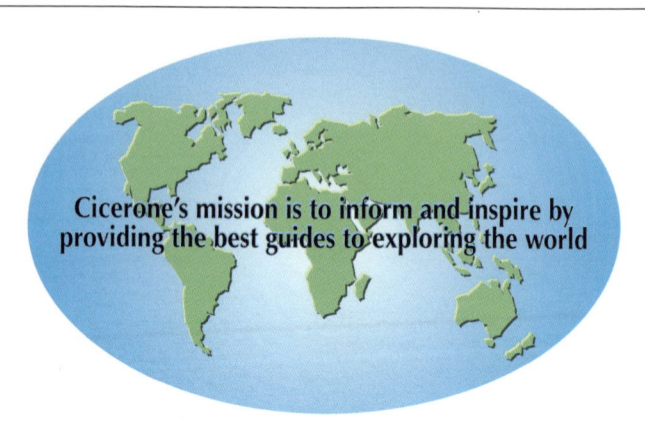

Cicerone's mission is to inform and inspire by providing the best guides to exploring the world

Since its foundation over 30 years ago, Cicerone has specialised in publishing guidebooks and has built a reputation for quality and reliability. It now publishes nearly 300 guides to the major destinations for outdoor enthusiasts, including Europe, UK and the rest of the world.

Written by leading and committed specialists, Cicerone guides are recognised as the most authoritative. They are full of information, maps and illustrations so that the user can plan and complete a successful and safe trip or expedition – be it a long face climb, a walk over Lakeland fells, an alpine traverse, a Himalayan trek or a ramble in the countryside.

With a thorough introduction to assist planning, clear diagrams, maps and colour photographs to illustrate the terrain and route, and accurate and detailed text, Cicerone guides are designed for ease of use and access to the information.

If the facts on the ground change, or there is any aspect of a guide that you think we can improve, we are always delighted to hear from you.

Cicerone Press
2 Police Square Milnthorpe Cumbria LA7 7PY
Tel:01539 562 069   Fax:01539 563 417
e-mail:info@cicerone.co.uk   web:www.cicerone.co.uk

CICERONE